P9-BIZ-736

Vegan DINER

CLASSIC COMFORT FOOD
★ for the Body & Soul ★

Julie Hasson

RUNNING PRESS
PHILADELPHIA · LONDON

Copyright © 2011 by Julie Hasson

Photographs © 2011 by Steve Legato

All rights reserved under the Pan-American and International Copyright Conventions

Printed in China

This book may not be reproduced in whole or in part, in any form or by any
means, electronic or mechanical, including photocopying, recording, or by
any information storage and retrieval system now known or hereafter
invented, without written permission from the publisher.

9 8 7 6 5 4 3 2 1

Digit on the right indicates the number of this printing

Library of Congress Control Number: 2010925946

ISBN 978-0-7624-3784-9

Cover and interior design by Amanda Richmond
Edited by Kristen Green Wiewora

Special thanks to Silk City Diner, located at 435 Spring Garden Street in Philadelphia,
for graciously allowing our photographer to shoot inside the restaurant. Additional thanks to
Crate & Barrel, King of Prussia, PA; Scarlett Alley, Philadelphia, PA; and Open House,
Philadelphia, PA for loaning dinnerware, flatware, and table linens for the photographs.

Typography: Brownstone, Gotham, and Lomba

Running Press Book Publishers
2300 Chestnut Street
Philadelphia, PA 19103-4371

Visit us on the web!
www.runningpresscooks.com

To Jay,
my partner in crime

Contents

Acknowledgments

First and foremost, I want to thank my awesome husband Jay. Without you, I would not be able to do what I do. I am so incredibly lucky to have you in my life! You are always there cheering me on, making me laugh, picking up the slack when I go deep into my recipe-testing zone, listening to me talk endlessly about food, taste-testing (even when you're not in the mood), and just being an all-around groovy guy. I love you!

A giant thank you to my incredible children, Sydney and Noah. You guys rock! I am eternally grateful for your taste-testing, recipe suggestions, and patience while I was "buried" in the kitchen. I love you guys!

I also want to thank everyone involved with putting this book together. Lisa Ekus, my stellar super-agent, it's always a pleasure working with you. Kristen Green Wiewora, my editor at Running Press, for truly believing in this project and making everything come together so beautifully. Jane Falla, who not only believed in this book, but helped me put together a fantastic proposal. Steve Legato for your photos, Virginia Villalon for your great proofreading and copyediting, and Amanda Richmond for making this book look so cool.

Mom, thank you for introducing me to tofu, home-grown vegetables, homemade bread, asparagus soup, and for sharing your love and enthusiasm of food. You're the best! Jon, thank you for being an awesome brother, always "talking food", with me, and of course, always making me laugh. Dad and Ellen, thank you for your love and support, and Dad for passing on that dish-obsession gene. Louie, thank you for your love and support.

I also wish to thank Bryanna Clark Grogan, for introducing me to so many wonderful vegan recipes as I first embarked on my vegan journey. You paved the way for a whole new generation of vegan cuisine. And last but not least, thank you to my wonderful crew of taste-testers, who so enthusiastically tested out these recipes, always giving me your honest feedback: Donald Blum, Gabrielle Pope, Jenny Howard, Thalia Palmer, Ana Cruz, Aimee Kluiber, Arine Mentink, Jenni Mischel, Kim Lahn, Jeff Klein, and Sheree Britt. A big thank you to Bob's Red Mill, Earth Balance, Madhava, Butler Foods, Freddy Guy's Hazelnuts, and Nielsen-Massey Vanillas for generously sharing products for the testing of these recipes.

❖ ❖

Introduction

◆ ◆

Welcome to Vegan Diner! Come on in, grab a swivel seat at the counter and order yourself a cup of joe.

Diner food is as American as apple pie. My memories of dinner out usually meant eating at a favorite neighborhood diner. We all have one or maybe even two favorite places. I have very fond memories of being squished into slippery Naugahyde booths, with my grandmother on one side and my pesky little brother (forgive me Jon) on the other. It was where we could order pancakes for dinner, or a blue plate special slathered in gravy. From the moment I entered the diner, my attention was drawn to the tantalizing array of glistening berry pies, huge slabs of chocolate cake, and perfect parfait glasses layered with chocolate pudding and clouds of billowy whipped cream. No matter how full I was from dinner, I was a master at making room for dessert.

So it was of no surprise to me that I found myself veganizing diner specialties as my diet changed from vegetarian to vegan. I love food too much to not enjoy a stack of hotcakes dripping in maple syrup or a plate of biscuits and gravy, meatloaf and mashed potatoes, or a big slice of banana cream pie. No way, I love my comfort food too much!

As I conducted cooking classes over the past couple of years, students would always say to me "I would think about going vegan, but I love gravy too much," or "My doctor told me that I need to cut meat, dairy, and eggs out of my diet and I don't know how I'll ever live without my comfort food." I would always follow with "But you don't have to give up your favorite foods. You just need to learn to make them in a new way!" So it became my mission to develop diner-style recipes and comfort food favorites that have all of the wonderful flavors and creamy textures that we all love, done with a vegan twist.

I loved the challenge of cooking vegetarian meals. You quickly learn that one cannot live on peanut butter sandwiches and bean burritos alone. The real fun began in creating vegan recipes for my friend, Heather, when she came over for dinner. It had been easy for me to rely on eggs and dairy in my diet, but I soon realized that there were many other ways to achieve similar results.

So as they say, the rest is history. After giving up dairy, eggs came next. I quickly learned that scrambled tofu for breakfast can be just as fab as eggs (if not better!) and that baking without eggs is totally doable. Although we're taught that pancakes, cakes, and cookies need eggs for structure, this is not necessarily true. Through trial and error I learned that in addition to commercial egg replacers, soy flour, ground flax, and soy yogurt make excellent egg replacers. In fact, sometimes you don't even need a substitute at all. The kitchen became my laboratory and I set out to learn as much as I could.

Let's just say that through all of the experimentation, transformations, and recipe veganizations, the delicious diner-style comfort food of my youth has been recreated exactly as I remember. The food that we all grew up on and enjoyed in those springy Naugahyde booths has merely been transformed. The recipes in this book can be used across the board from quick weeknight meals to weekend brunch to Thanksgiving and holiday get-togethers. I hope that you enjoy these recipes as much as I do so a piece of our nostalgic past will continue to live on, with fond memories of people, places, and great food.

Good Eats!

The Vegan Pantry

Agar Powder: Also sometimes referred to as agar-agar. Agar is a seaweed product that is used to gel liquids. It is used in place of gelatin (which is derived from animals). Agar is rich in calcium. The powder, which is what I use, is much more concentrated than agar flakes. They are not interchangeable.

Agave Syrup: A natural sweetener made from the agave plant. Agave has a color, consistency, and taste similar to honey, and comes in both light and amber. I really like Madhava and Wholesome Sweeteners, two brand names of agave.

Bouillon Cubes: Vegan bouillon cubes are great for flavoring broths, soups, seitan, etc. Check the ingredients to make sure the ingredients are vegan. A few brands to look for are Rapunzel Vegetable Bouillon Cubes and Harvest 2000 International Vegetarian Chicken Flavor Bouillon Powder. They are usually available in well-stocked grocery and health food stores or on the Internet.

Bragg: Also known as Bragg Liquid Aminos. It is made from soybeans and has a taste that is similar to soy sauce. Look for Bragg in well-stocked health food stores or on the Internet.

Chipotle Pepper: Made from red ripe jalapeños that have been slow smoked. Chipotles have a deep, smoky flavor.

Chocolate: Look for dairy-free varieties of dark and semisweet chocolate and chocolate chips. Many brands are now fair trade and organic, too.

Citrus Oils: These are fabulous natural flavorings, which I adore! They are made from pressed fresh limes, lemons, oranges, and tangerines (depending on which variety you buy.) It is 100% pure, with a bright citrus flavor. I love the Boyajian brand.

Cocoa Powder: Look for Dutch process, a dark rich cocoa powder processed with alkali, which neutralizes its natural acidity.

Cornstarch: A thickening agent made from corn.

Egg Replacer: A powdered product to use in place of eggs in baked goods. You can't make meringues with it, but it is very effective in cakes and cookies. Two great brands are Bob's Red Mill and Ener-G Foods, both available in well-stocked health food stores. I also like to use ground flax meal or soy flour as an egg replacer in recipes.

Flaxseed Oil: A great vegetarian source of omega-3 fatty acids. You don't want to heat flax oil. Use it in salad dressings or drizzled on food.

Flour: I use primarily unbleached wheat flour in my baked goods, although in some recipes I also call for cake flour, whole wheat flour, white wheat flour, whole wheat pastry flour, oat flour, chickpea or garbanzo bean flour, and spelt flour. Look for specialty flours in well-stocked grocery or health food stores or online. I especially like the wonderful flours from Bob's Red Mill and used their flours for the recipes in this book.

Instant Yeast: Once I started using instant yeast I became hooked. I particularly like the SAF® brand, although there are several brands on the market. Instant yeast is very easy to use (no need to proof or pre-dissolve your yeast). It's also fast-acting and very reliable, even for beginners. Look for instant yeast in inexpensive one-pound packages found in club stores, online, or from restaurant suppliers. Keep your yeast in the freezer in an airtight container. It will stay fresh for up to two years. Instant yeast is sometimes sold as quick yeast or rapid-rise active dry yeast.

Liquid Smoke: Liquid smoke adds a wonderfully smoky flavor to recipes. It is in fact vegan and natural, although check the ingredient label because some varieties add unnecessary ingredients.

Malt Powder: Powdered malt extract is a non-diastatic barley malt, which is made from the evaporated concentrate of barley malt (check the packaging for the correct variety). The malt extract can also be used as a natural sweetener. Look for it in natural foods stores and online.

Margarine: Look for a good-tasting, vegan, non-hydrogenated margarine such as Earth Balance® brand. Margarine can be used almost interchangeably when a recipe calls for butter, especially when a buttery taste is required.

Milks: There are many different varieties of non-dairy milks. Look for almond milk, hemp milk, oat milk, hazelnut milk, rice milk, coconut milk, and soymilk. Also look for organic varieties in vanilla, chocolate, plain, and unsweetened. Soymilk works well in baking and cooking. Use plain unsweetened soymilk for savory cooking. The flavor can vary from brand to brand, so I recommend conducting your own taste test to see which brands you prefer. Non-dairy milks can be found both refrigerated and shelf-stable in most grocery stores.

Millet: A small, quick-cooking grain. Millet is high in protein and gluten free.

Nutritional Yeast Flakes: Dried flakes derived from yeast. They are are high in B vitamins, protein, and minerals. Nutritional yeast also acts as a flavor enhancer in food. I especially love Red Star® brand.

Oats: A whole grain that is usually purchased "rolled." Buy quick-cooking and old-fashioned varieties to use in desserts, bread, and granola. You can also grind the oats into fluffy flour, using a blender, for use as a thickener in gravy.

Poultry Seasoning: A must-use spice blend in the vegan kitchen! This is a savory blend of herbs and spices, which typically includes thyme, sage, marjoram, rosemary, black pepper, and nutmeg.

Quinoa: An ancient grain that is quick cooking, this complete protein is packed with vitamins and minerals.

Salt: All of the recipes in this book were tested with fine sea salt.

Smoked Paprika: Also known as pimentón or Spanish paprika. When used in cooking, it imparts a wonderful smoky flavor to food.

Soy Crumbles: Look for soy crumbles in packages in the refrigerated section of well-stocked grocery and health food stores. I like the Yves brand Meatless Ground Round Original. You can also find soy or veggie crumbles in the freezer section of grocery stores.

Soy Curls™: A delicious and versatile product made from whole, non-GMO soybeans. These come in dried strips, and simply need to be reconstituted in hot broth or water for 10 minutes. They are available online and in some health food stores.

Soy Yogurt: Non-dairy yogurt made from soymilk. There are a number of different brands out on the market. Two of my favorite brands are WholeSoy & Co. and Wildwood. Soy yogurt works really well in vegan desserts and baked goods. Soy yogurt is usually too sweet for savory recipes.

Spelt Flour: Spelt is an ancient variety of wheat, with a delicious nutty flavor. It is not gluten free.

Sugar: Not all sugars are vegan, as cane sugar is sometimes filtered through bone char (from animals). Beet sugar (granulated white and brown) and organic sugars are processed without the use of bone char.

Tahini: Hulled and toasted sesame seeds that have been ground into a paste. It's rich in calcium and protein, and is most often used in hummus.

Tempeh: A fermented soy product that is high in protein. Tempeh has a chewy, nutty flavor.

Tofu: Made from soymilk, a high-quality source of protein. Tofu comes in many different varieties, from silken to extra firm. Silken is usually best blended in desserts, dressings, or creamy sauces. Firm and extra-firm water-packed tofu (not silken) works best for grilling, sautéing, and other savory applications.

TVP or TSP: Textured vegetable protein or textured soy protein, (essentially the same thing). They're made from defatted soy flour. It's low in fat, high in protein, and cooks quickly.

Vanilla: Always use pure vanilla, never artificial! I use and love the vanilla from Nielsen-Massey. They also carry a vanilla paste, which is incredible, with little flecks of the vanilla bean.

Vegetable Shortening: When I use vegetable shortening in a recipe, I like to use organic palm shortening, such as Spectrum brand.

Vegan Cream Cheese and Sour Cream: There are a couple of brands of vegan cream cheese and sour cream now on the market. My first choice is Tofutti, which is what I used for testing recipes in this book. I like Follow Your Heart® brand, too, which also makes a delicious mayonnaise called Vegenaise®.

Vital Wheat Gluten: This stuff is amazing! It is simply the pure protein from wheat, which gives mock meats their wonderfully chewy texture. It comes as a flour (although don't confuse it with gluten flour which is something different), and can be purchased in bags or bulk bins at some supermarkets, health food stores, and online. Not all brands work well in seitan recipes. I highly recommend Bob's Red Mill, which is what I used for developing and testing these recipes.

Xanthan Gum: Used to add volume and viscosity to gluten-free bread and baked goods. It can also be used as a thickener.

SPECIAL EQUIPMENT

◆ ◆ ◆ ◆ ◆ ◆ ◆ ◆ ◆ ◆ ◆

Blender: This really helps in the vegan kitchen, from blending cashews into a silken cream to whipping silken tofu into a luscious mousse. There are several brands that I have used and loved over the years, including the famous Vita-Mix and Blendtec's Total Blender models. Power and wattage does make a difference when it comes to a blender.

Cookie/Ice Cream Scoops: These are available in a variety of sizes, and are one of my secrets for perfect cookies. Use scoops to measure batter so that your cookies and muffins will bake evenly, come out the same size, and look bakery-perfect every time!

Cooling Rack: Elevates the baking pan or baked goods so that air can circulate around it.

Dry Metal Measuring Cups: This is the most accurate way to measure dry ingredients (with the exception of a digital scale), and the way that I always measure my flour. Always spoon your flour or dry ingredients into the cup and level the top by scraping across with the flat side of a knife (or skewer). This will give you an accurate measurement.

Food Processor: This machine is essential for chopping vegetables and nuts, blending tofu, and a million other things! I recommend the Cuisinart or KitchenAid brands, as they will last for years and do a more consistent job than less expensive brands.

Ice Cream Maker: Once you try your hand at making vegan ice cream at home, you will never want store-bought again! I tested the ice cream recipes in this book on two different Cuisinart models, and both were fabulous. One of the models uses a separate bowl, which is first frozen overnight, and the other model has a built-in compressor so that no pre-freezing is necessary.

Immersion/Stick Blender: I love immersion blenders. They blend ingredients quickly with a minimum of mess. They are great for blending sauces, dressings, and whipped cream.

Liquid Measuring Cups: The most accurate way to measure liquid ingredients is in glass or plastic liquid measuring cups with a lip or spout. I like to keep a variety of different sizes in my kitchen for baking.

Metal Measuring Spoons: This is the most accurate way to measure small amounts of both liquid and dry ingredients.

Microplane Zester/Grater: A handy tool for quickly removing and grating citrus zest. They also work well for grating cinnamosticks, whole nutmeg, garlic, and ginger.

Mixing Bowls: A nesting set (or two or

three) of mixing bowls is a must in the dessert kitchen. I like to have both stainless steel and ceramic, depending on the mixing job. Stainless steel works better for whipping cream, ceramic for cookie or cake batters.

Oil: I generally use canola oil for baking and olive oil for cooking. I find that not only does canola oil have a mild flavor, but cookies actually come out softer and fluffier. Both oils come in organic varieties. For deep-frying, I generally use vegetable oil.

Oven: Make sure your oven is calibrated (precisely adjusted) so that it bakes evenly and at the required temperature. I also recommend using an oven thermometer, so you know the exact temperature of the oven. The recipes in this book were tested using a conventional gas oven.

Parchment Paper: A grease and heat-resistant paper used to line baking pans. It keeps your baked goods from sticking and burning (unless you over-bake them of course!) and makes clean-up a breeze.

Sifter or Strainer: This works well for sifting dry ingredients, or dusting a dessert with powdered sugar.

Silicone Spatulas: The new silicone spatulas are heatproof to 600 F. They are a boon to bakers, as they will scrape a bowl clean with ease. They are dishwasher safe and can be used for stovetop cooking as well.

Silpat® Silicone Pan Liners: A fabulous nonstick baking mat that fits on top of your baking sheet. Used in place of parchment paper, it is heat resistant up to 480 F, making any baking sheet nonstick.

Stand Mixer: This isn't a must for all recipes, but it sure makes life a lot easier. I recommend a heavy, sturdy stand mixer, and have used a Cuisinart, KitchenAid, and Bosch, all with fabulous results. It will last for years and makes baking a snap!

Whisk: A great tool for whipping or whisking both liquid and dry ingredients. I like to use it to mix together and aerate dry ingredients in recipes, as well as for emulsifying dressings and sauces.

◆ ◆

HELPFUL COOKING and BAKING TIPS

◆ ◆ ◆ ◆ ◆ ◆ ◆ ◆ ◆ ◆ ◆ ◆ ◆ ◆ ◆ ◆ ◆ ◆ ◆

• Read the entire recipe through before starting. This way you know both the steps and ingredients in the recipe before you start.

• Make sure that your oven is properly preheated before baking. It will probably take between 10 to 15 minutes to preheat, depending on your oven.

• When measuring dry ingredients, always spoon into dry measuring cups or spoons, and level the top by scraping across with the flat side of a knife (or skewer).

• If baking more than one cake or tray of cookies at a time, rotate your baking sheets halfway through baking.

• If baking multiple desserts (or trays of cookies) at a time, the baking time will take longer. Adjust your baking time accordingly, relying on visual signs of doneness.

• A fine-mesh strainer makes a quick and fabulous flour sifter.

• Make sure that your biscuits and cookies are evenly spaced on the pan to allow room for spreading and rising.

• Use a cookie scoop for a professional appearance with your biscuits, cookies, or muffins. They will also bake more evenly if they are all the same size.

• Cook a big pot of brown rice, quinoa, or other grain, so that you have leftovers on hand to use for veggie burgers. The same goes for cooking beans, too. Both cooked grains and beans can be frozen as well.

• When my kitchen is chilly in the winter, it can make bread baking a very slow proposition. The dough rises best in a warmer environment. So when it's chilly indoors, I let my dough rise on top of the stove while it's preheating. Sometimes it just needs a little warmth to get it going. I've even been known to let my dough rise near the fireplace. Whatever it takes!

• Have fun!

Breakfast

Cherry–Almond–Poppyseed Muffins

This muffin recipe is adapted from a non–vegan
cousin that we used to sell at Babycakes, our wholesale bakery in Los Angeles.
Along with blueberry, it was a year–round favorite. Who knew back then that
muffins could be so scrumptious and easily made without eggs and butter?

MAKES 12 MUFFINS

2 cups all-purpose flour

2 tablespoons poppy seeds

1 tablespoon flaxseed meal, preferably golden

1 tablespoon baking powder

$1/8$ teaspoon fine sea salt

$3/4$ cup plus 1 tablespoon granulated sugar, divided

1 cup soymilk, divided

$1/3$ cup canola oil

$1/4$ cup unsweetened apple-sauce

2 teaspoons pure almond extract

$2/3$ cup dried cherries

Preheat oven to 350°F. Line a 12-cup muffin tray with paper liners or grease well with vegetable shortening or nonstick cooking spray.

In a medium bowl, whisk the flour, poppyseeds, flax meal, baking powder, and salt, mixing well.

In a large bowl, whisk together $3/4$ cup sugar, half of the soymilk, canola oil, applesauce, and almond extract, whisking until smooth. Add the flour mixture a little at a time, alternating with the remaining soymilk, whisking just until combined. Stir in the dried cherries.

Scoop the batter evenly amongst the 12 cups of the prepared muffin pan and sprinkle remaining table-spoon of sugar over the tops of the muffins.

Bake for 20 to 25 minutes, or until muffins are just barely golden around the edges and a tester inserted into the center comes out clean.

Let muffins cool in the pan for 5 minutes, and remove to a rack to cool completely.

Variation: You can substitute dried cranberries for the cherries.

Poppyseeds can go rancid quickly, and are best stored in an airtight container in the freezer.

Blueberry Nutmeg Muffins

Blueberry muffins were one of the first things I started baking in elementary school. They were easy to make, bursting with the goodness of ripe blueberries, and topped with nutmeg and sugar. This recipe is adapted from my special bakery recipe, which I used to bake by the hundreds.

MAKES 12 MUFFINS

2 cups all-purpose flour

1 tablespoon flaxseed meal, preferably golden

1 tablespoon baking powder

2 teaspoons freshly grated nutmeg, divided

$1/8$ teaspoon fine sea salt

$3/4$ cup plus 1 tablespoon granulated sugar, divided

$1^1/4$ cups soymilk, divided

$1/3$ cup canola oil

2 teaspoons pure vanilla extract

1 cup fresh or frozen blue-berries (not thawed)

Preheat oven to 350°F. Line a 12-cup muffin tray with paper liners or grease the pan.

In a medium bowl, combine the flour, flax meal, baking powder, $1^1/2$ teaspoons grated nutmeg, and salt, mixing well.

In a large bowl, whisk together $3/4$ cup sugar, half of the soymilk, canola oil, and vanilla, until smooth. Alternately add the flour mixture and remaining soymilk, a little at a time, whisking just until mixed. Stir in the blue-berries.

In a small bowl, mix together the remaining 1 table-spoon sugar and $1/2$ teaspoon grated nutmeg.

Scoop the batter into prepared pan, dividing the bat-ter evenly among the 12 cups, filling them $3/4$ of the way full. Sprinkle the sugar and nutmeg mixture over top of the muffins.

Bake the muffins in the preheated oven for 20 to 30 minutes, or until the tops are puffed and a tester inserted into the center comes out clean.

Let the muffins cool in the pan for 5 minutes, and remove to a rack to cool to room temperature.

Variation: For apricot blueberry muffins, add about $1/3$ cup chopped dried apricots to the batter along with the blueberries.

Mocha Muffins

Nothing will jumpstart your morning like these Mocha Muffins.
Rich with the flavor of espresso and cinnamon, you'll find yourself making them again and again.

MAKES 12 MUFFINS

2 cups unbleached all-purpose flour

1 tablespoon flax meal, preferably golden flax

2 tablespoons finely grated espresso or French roast coffee

1 tablespoon baking powder

1 teaspoon ground cinnamon

$1/8$ teaspoon fine sea salt

$3/4$ cup granulated sugar

1 cup vanilla soymilk

$1/3$ cup canola oil

1 tablespoon pure vanilla extract

$1/4$ cup brewed coffee, cooled

$1/2$ cup semisweet chocolate chips

Preheat oven to 350°F. Line a 12-cup muffin tray with paper liners or grease the pan with vegetable shortening.

In a medium bowl, combine the flour, flax meal, ground espresso, baking powder, cinnamon, and salt, mixing well.

In a large bowl, whisk together the sugar, soymilk, oil, and vanilla, until smooth. Add the flour mixture and brewed coffee, whisking just until mixed. Stir in the chocolate chips.

Divide the batter evenly among the 12 cups in the pan, filling each $3/4$ of the way full. Bake the muffins in the preheated oven for 20 to 30 minutes, or until the tops are puffed and a tester inserted into the center comes out clean.

Let the muffins cool in the pan for 5 minutes, and remove to a rack to cool to room temperature.

You can make your own flax meal for these muffins, by grinding whole flaxseeds in a blender or coffee grinder. Since there's coffee in the recipe, you don't even need to clean off the blades first!

Variation: If you want your muffins to have a hint of orange flavor, add about $1/4$ teaspoon pure orange oil to the batter in addition to the coffee.

Apple Spice Coffee Cake

Coffee cake and cooked apples are two of my favorite things.
This coffee cake combines the two, and is perfect for breakfast with a big mug of coffee or chai tea.

MAKES ONE
8 X 8-INCH PAN

2 cups all-purpose flour

2 tablespoons soy flour

2 teaspoons baking powder

1/2 teaspoon freshly grated nutmeg

1/4 teaspoon fine sea salt

1/2 cup canola oil

1 cup packed light brown sugar

2 teaspoons pure vanilla extract

1 cup almond or soymilk

3 tablespoons granulated sugar

1/2 teaspoon ground cinnamon

1 large or 2 small Granny Smith apples peeled, cored, and thinly sliced

Preheat oven to 350°F. Grease an 8-inch square glass baking dish with shortening.

In a small bowl, sift together the flour, soy flour, baking powder, grated nutmeg and salt.

In a large bowl, beat together the oil, brown sugar, and vanilla with an electric mixer. Add the flour mixture a little at a time, alternating with the almond milk, beating until just combined.

In a small bowl combine granulated sugar with the cinnamon.

Spread half the batter into the prepared baking dish. Lay the apple slices on top of the batter. It's okay if some slices overlap. Sprinkle half of the cinnamon-sugar mixture over apples. Spread the rest of the batter over the apples. Sprinkle the remaining cinnamon-sugar on top.

Bake the cake for 50 to 60 minutes, or until cake is golden-brown, and a tester inserted into center of cake comes out clean. Remove to a rack to cool completely before serving.

I like to use a glass baking dish for baking cakes. An added bonus is that you can serve the finished cake right from the pan. Plus, I love the old-fashioned look of glass.

Cinnamon Orange Rolls

These cinnamon rolls are the bomb, baby!

If you want to win friends and influence people, this recipe is your ticket. If you can't find the soymilk powder, you can omit it and substitute $1/2$ cup soymilk for the water.

MAKES 12 ROLLS

Dough

1 package ($2^1/_4$ teaspoons) active dry yeast

1 teaspoon granulated sugar

$1/_4$ cup hot water (110 to 115°F)

$1/_4$ cup agave nectar

$1/_4$ cup canola oil

$1/_4$ cup orange juice

$1/_2$ cup water, room temperature

1 tablespoon orange zest

$3^3/_4$ to 4 cups unbleached all-purpose flour

2 tablespoons soymilk powder (*see next page*)

1 teaspoon fine sea salt

Filling

3 tablespoons non-hydrogenated vegan margarine, softened

$2/_3$ cup packed light brown sugar

1 teaspoon ground cinnamon

Glaze

2 cups confectioners' sugar

3 tablespoons orange juice, preferably fresh-squeezed

Grease a 13 x 9-inch glass baking dish well with vegetable shortening.

For the dough: In a small bowl, combine the yeast, sugar, and hot water, stirring to mix. Set aside for 10 minutes, until foamy.

In a large measuring cup, whisk together the agave nectar, canola oil, orange juice, remaining $1/2$ cup water, and orange zest and set aside.

In the bowl of a stand mixer fitted with the paddle, combine the flour, soymilk powder, and salt. Beat on low until mixed. Add the reserved yeast and agave mixture to the flour, and beat until the dough forms a ball. Switch the paddle to the dough hook, and let the machine knead the dough for about 3 to 5 minutes, or until the dough looks silky. The dough should be soft and smooth, not sticky. If the dough is sticky, add more flour, a tablespoon at a time.

Place the dough in a large lightly oiled bowl, covering with plastic wrap. Let the dough rise until doubled, about 1 hour.

On a lightly floured surface, roll the dough into a rectangle, approximately 16 x 12 inches.

For the filling: Spread the softened margarine over the dough, leaving a $1/2$-inch border on all sides. Sprinkle the brown sugar over the margarine. Sprinkle the cinnamon over the brown sugar. Starting with the long edge, roll the dough up into a spiral, jelly-roll style. Pinch the edges together to seal. Carefully cut the roll into 12 equal pieces. Place the rolls into the prepared baking dish. Cover with plastic wrap and let rise for 30 minutes (or until rolls are almost doubled in size).

Preheat the oven to 350°F.

Remove plastic wrap and bake the rolls for 30 to 35 minutes, or until firm to the touch and lightly golden. Remove baking dish from oven and set aside on a rack to cool slightly.

For the glaze: While the rolls are cooling, whisk the confectioners' sugar and orange juice in a medium bowl, until smooth. Drizzle the glaze over the warm rolls and serve.

Variation: To make this dough in the food processor, combine the flour, soymilk powder, and salt in the work bowl, fitted with the metal blade. Pulse the flour until mixed. Add the reserved yeast and agave mixture to the flour, and process until the dough forms a ball. Pulse the dough another 4 to 5 times, until the dough looks silky.

If you can find the soymilk powder, it works really well in bread dough to give it a soft texture. I use the Better Than Milk brand. Look for it in health food stores or online.

Banana Biscuits

A lightly sweet biscuit, with the nutty flavor of wheat
and little bursts of banana. They are almost like a cross between a
scone and a traditional biscuit, and are a delicious way to start the day.

MAKES 9

2 cups whole wheat
pastry flour

$1/3$ cup packed light brown
sugar

2 tablespoons baking
powder

$1/8$ teaspoon fine sea salt

$1/2$ cup almond milk or
soymilk

1 teaspoon pure vanilla
extract

$1/3$ cup canola oil

1 banana, cut into quarters
lengthwise and diced

$1^1/2$ teaspoons granulated
sugar

$1/4$ teaspoon ground
cinnamon

Preheat oven to 400°F. Line a baking sheet with parchment paper or a silicone mat.

In a large bowl, sift together the whole wheat flour, brown sugar, baking powder, and salt.

Add the milk, vanilla, canola oil, and banana to the flour mixture and stir just until the mixture comes together, and is thick and sticky. Scoop nine rounded balls of dough onto the prepared baking sheet.

In a small cup, mix together the granulated sugar and cinnamon. Sprinkle on top of the biscuits.

Bake in preheated oven for 20 minutes, or until lightly browned. Cool on a cooling rack.

These biscuits are best served the same day that they are made. If you find yourself with a few left over the next day, I highly recommend warming them in a toaster oven (not the microwave), and serving with a little vegan margarine, if desired.

Banana Chocolate Chip Bread

Banana breads have been a staple in my family for years,

from my mom's special recipe as a child to baking them by the hundreds at our bakery. It took me a while to come up with a vegan version: tender, loaded with banana flavor, and studded with chocolate chips. This bread is even better than the original.

MAKES ONE
9 X 5-INCH LOAF

2 cups all-purpose flour

1 tablespoon flaxseed meal, preferably golden

2 teaspoons baking powder

$^1/_2$ teaspoon baking soda

$^1/_4$ teaspoon fine sea salt

$^2/_3$ cup packed light brown sugar

$^1/_2$ cup canola oil

1 cup puréed ripe bananas (about 2 large bananas)

1 tablespoon pure vanilla extract

$^1/_2$ cup almond milk or soymilk

$^1/_2$ cup semisweet chocolate chips

Preheat oven to 350°F. Grease a 9 x 5-inch metal loaf pan really well with shortening.

In a medium bowl, whisk together the flour, flax meal, baking powder, baking soda, and salt, mixing well.

In a large bowl, whisk together the brown sugar, canola oil, puréed banana, and vanilla until smooth. Add the flour mixture and almond milk, whisking just until mixed. Stir in the chocolate chips.

Scoop the batter into the prepared pan and bake in the preheated oven for 60 minutes, or until the bread is puffed in center and firm to the touch, and a tester inserted into the center comes out clean.

Let the bread cool in the pan for 10 minutes, and remove to a rack to cool completely.

Don't forget to measure the banana in a liquid measuring cup after puréeing. This way you'll get a more accurate measurement and your bread will come out beautifully. This bread freezes well.

Carrot Pineapple Loaf Cake

A taste of the tropics, with a lovely light texture
and lots of shredded carrots and pineapple thrown in for good measure.
Try serving this cake with a smear of non–dairy cream cheese.

MAKES ONE
9 X 5–INCH LOAF

1 cup unbleached all-
purpose flour

1 cup whole wheat pastry
flour

2 tablespoons ground
flaxseed meal (preferably
golden flax)

2 teaspoons baking powder

1 teaspoon ground
cinnamon

Scant $\frac{1}{4}$ teaspoon fine
sea salt

$\frac{1}{2}$ cup canola oil

1 cup firmly packed light
brown sugar

$\frac{1}{2}$ cup canned, crushed
pineapple, juice drained
and reserved

$\frac{1}{2}$ cup pineapple juice

$\frac{1}{2}$ cup unsweetened
applesauce

1 lightly packed cup shredded, peeled carrots (about
1 jumbo carrot)

Preheat oven to 350°F. Line a 9 x 5-inch metal loaf pan with parchment paper and grease well with vegetable shortening. This cake can have a tendency to stick if not greased and lined well.

In a medium bowl, combine the all-purpose flour, whole wheat flour, flax meal, baking powder, cinnamon, and salt, mixing well.

In a large bowl, whisk together the canola oil, brown sugar, pineapple, pineapple juice, and applesauce. Add the flour mixture, stirring just until mixed. Stir in the shredded carrots.

Pour the batter into the prepared pan and bake in the preheated oven for 55 to 65 minutes, or until top springs back when touched, and a tester inserted into the center comes out clean.

Let the cake cool in the pan for 10 minutes, and remove to a rack to cool to room temperature.

This cake can be embellished even further by adding $\frac{1}{2}$ cup raisins, flaked or shredded coconut, or chopped walnuts to the batter.

Blueberry Loaf Cake with Lemon Glaze

Sometimes the simplest cakes are the best.

To me, nothing tops a big slice of blueberry loaf cake, especially this one which is garnished with a delectable lemon glaze. You can also omit the blueberries for a fantastic lemon loaf cake. I promise you that no one would guess that this cake is vegan!

MAKES ONE
9 X 5-INCH LOAF

Cake

2 cups unbleached all-purpose flour

3 tablespoons soy flour

2 teaspoons baking powder

$1/8$ teaspoon fine sea salt

1 cup granulated sugar

1 cup soymilk, divided

$1/3$ cup canola oil

3 tablespoons freshly squeezed lemon juice

Finely grated lemon zest from $1^{1}/_{2}$ lemons

$^{3}/_{4}$ teaspoon pure lemon oil or $1^{1}/_{4}$ teaspoons pure lemon extract

1 cup fresh or frozen blueberries (do not thaw)

Glaze

1 cup confectioners' sugar

$1^{1}/_{2}$ to 2 tablespoons fresh lemon juice, or as needed

Preheat oven to 350°F. Line a 9 x 5-inch metal loaf pan with parchment paper and grease really well with vegetable shortening.

For the cake: In a medium bowl, combine the flour, soy flour, baking powder, and salt, mixing well.

In a large bowl, whisk together the sugar, half of the soymilk, canola oil, lemon juice, lemon zest, and lemon oil until smooth. Add the flour mixture and the remaining soymilk and lemon zest, whisking just until mixed. Stir in the blueberries.

Scoop the batter into the prepared pan and bake in the preheated oven for 55 to 65 minutes, or until top of cake is puffed with a crack down the center, and a tester inserted into the center comes out clean.

Let the cake cool in the pan for 10 minutes, and remove to a rack to cool to room temperature.

For the glaze: While the cake is cooling, in a medium bowl combine the confectioners' sugar and lemon juice. With a whisk or an electric mixer, beat the glaze until smooth. If mixture is too thick, add another teaspoon or two of lemon juice as needed. Drizzle the glaze over the top of the cooled cake to serve.

Tip: Don't be tempted to substitute ground flax for the soy flour called for in this recipe. The soy flour helps this rise into one gorgeous cake!

Mocha Java Cake

For years I have had people beg me for this recipe

(albeit the egg and dairy version), which had a sort of cult following back in my bakery days.
I am still amazed that I was able to veganize it, and it's every bit as delicious as the original.

MAKES ONE
9 X 5-INCH LOAF

1 cup plus 2 tablespoons
soymilk, heated to steam-
ing and kept warm

1/4 cup finely ground
espresso or French roast
coffee

2 tablespoons instant
coffee

2 cups all-purpose flour

4 tablespoons soy flour

2 teaspoons baking powder

2 teaspoons ground
cinnamon

1/4 teaspoon fine sea salt

1 1/2 cups granulated sugar

1 cup canola oil

1 tablespoon pure vanilla
extract

3/4 cup semisweet chocolate
chips

Preheat oven to 350°F. Line a 9 x 5-inch metal loaf pan with parchment paper and grease well with vegetable shortening. This cake can have a tendency to stick if not greased and lined well.

In a small bowl, whisk together the soymilk, espresso, and instant coffee until smooth. Set aside.

In a medium bowl, combine the flour, soy flour, baking powder, cinnamon, and salt, mixing well.

In a large bowl, combine the sugar, canola oil, and vanilla, whisking until smooth. Add the flour mixture to the bowl, alternating with the milk mixture, stirring just until mixed. Stir in the chocolate chips.

Scoop the batter into the prepared pan and bake in preheated oven for 60 to 70 minutes, or until the top of cake is puffed with a crack down the center, and a tester inserted into the center comes out clean.

Let the cake cool in the pan for 10 minutes, and remove to a rack to cool to room temperature.

This cake can tend to crumble a little when sliced, so make sure to cut thick slices.

Diner Granola

Granola is so easy to make at home,

and can be customized to your own personal tastes (don't like nuts? No worries!).
It's also very economical, too. So put away your boxed breakfast cereals, and start
your day with homemade cereal and your favorite non–dairy milk.

MAKES ABOUT 4 CUPS

3 cups old-fashioned rolled oats

$1/4$ cup packed light brown sugar

3 tablespoons flaxseed meal, preferably golden

$1^1/2$ teaspoons ground cinnamon

4 tablespoons canola oil

3 tablespoons agave nectar

1 teaspoon vanilla extract

$1/2$ cup hazelnuts, skinned and coarsely chopped

$1/3$ cup dried cherries or raisins, or dried fruit of your choice, chopped

Preheat oven to 325°F. Line a large baking sheet with parchment paper or a silicone mat.

In a large bowl, combine the oats, brown sugar, flaxseed meal, and cinnamon.

In a small bowl, mix together the canola oil, agave, and vanilla extract. Add the oil mixture to the oat mixture, mixing well until the oats are evenly coated.

Spread the oat mixture out in an even layer on the prepared baking sheet. Bake for about 20 minutes, stirring occasionally.

Remove the pan from the oven and add the hazelnuts. Bake granola for another 10 minutes, or until evenly browned (but not too dark or else it can become bitter).

Remove the pan again from the oven and add the dried cherries or raisins. Cool the pan on a rack, stirring occasionally until granola reaches room temperature. Transfer the granola to an airtight container and store at room temperature or in the refrigerator. I like to keep mine in a covered glass crock on the counter.

Variation: Substitute chopped walnuts or pecans for the hazelnuts. If you prefer your granola a little less sweet, you can reduce the brown sugar as needed.

Diner Donuts

There's nothing like fresh donuts, still warm with a
sweet glaze. I worked for months to come up with the perfect yeast–raised donuts,
which I was determined to do. I now present to you dear reader, the perfect vegan donut.
These donuts can either be glazed or dipped in cinnamon sugar: the choice is yours.

MAKES 12 DONUTS

Dough

1 package (2¼ teaspoons) active dry yeast

¼ cup plus 1 teaspoon granulated sugar, divided

¼ cup hot water (110 to 115°F)

About 4 to 4¼ cups unbleached all-purpose flour, plus more for dusting

3 tablespoons soymilk powder (*see tip, next page*)

1 teaspoon ground nutmeg

½ teaspoon fine sea salt

1 cup water, room temperature

¼ cup canola oil

4 cups vegetable or peanut oil, or more as needed for frying

For the dough: In a small bowl, combine the yeast, 1 tea-spoon sugar, and hot water. Set aside for 10 minutes, until foamy.

In the bowl of a stand mixer, combine 4 cups of the flour, the remaining ¼ cup of sugar, soymilk powder, nutmeg, and salt, and mix until combined. Add the reserved yeast, water, and canola oil to the flour, beating until the dough forms a ball. Continue beating the dough until it's soft and silky, not sticky. If the dough is too sticky, add more flour, a tablespoon at a time, up to ¼ cup.

Place the dough in a large lightly oiled bowl, covering with plastic wrap. Let dough rise until doubled, about 1 hour.

On a well-floured surface or on floured waxed paper, roll the dough out to ½-inch thick. Cut out the donuts using a 2½ to 3-inch donut cutter. Alternately use a 2½ to 3-inch biscuit cutter and a ⅞-inch cutter for the cen-ter hole. Set on a floured silicone mat or baking sheet, cover lightly with a kitchen towel, and let rise for 30 minutes, or until slightly puffed.

Fill a deep fryer or Dutch oven with about 3 inches of vegetable oil and heat to 365°F. Test the oil to check the frying temperature: pinch off a small piece of dough and carefully drop it in the oil. If it sizzles imme-diately with vigorous bubbles, it's ready. Adjust the heat as necessary to maintain the temperature; other-wise the oil will continue to heat. Once oil is hot, gently

(*continued on next page*)

Glaze

1 1/2 cups confectioners' sugar

3 tablespoons soymilk, or more as needed

1 teaspoon pure vanilla extract

Cinnamon–Sugar Topping

1/4 cup sugar

1/4 teaspoon ground cinnamon

place the donuts into the oil in batches without crowding them. Cook until lightly golden, about 1 minute. Carefully turn donuts over, and cook until golden on the second side. Transfer donuts to a baking sheet lined with paper towels to absorb the extra oil. Allow donuts to cool for 15 minutes before glazing or rolling in cinnamon sugar.

For glazed donuts: While donuts are cooling, in a medium bowl whisk together the confectioners' sugar, soymilk, and vanilla extract until smooth. Dip the tops of the cooled donuts in the glaze and set on a cooling rack for about 15 minutes before serving.

For cinnamon-sugar donuts: In a small bowl, mix together sugar and cinnamon. Dip hot donuts in cinnamon sugar and roll to coat completely. Place sugared donuts on a rack or plate until ready to serve.

Tip: If you don't have soymilk powder, you can substitute 1 cup of soymilk for the 1 cup of room temperature water, and omit the powder. This recipe gives you a choice of finishes for the donuts; you can roll them in cinnamon sugar or dip them in a glaze. Feel free to do some of each.

Crispy Banana–Cinnamon Waffles

The secret ingredient here is the crispy rice cereal,
which give the waffles a little extra crunch. With a light banana flavor and a hint
of cinnamon, it's hard to stop reaching for more.

MAKES ABOUT 11
BELGIAN-STYLE WAFFLES

1 cup whole wheat pastry flour

1 cup all-purpose flour

1/2 cup crispy rice cereal

4 teaspoons baking powder

1 teaspoon ground cinnamon

1/8 teaspoon fine sea salt

1 cup puréed ripe banana (about 2 bananas)

1 cup soymilk or almond milk, plus more as needed

1 tablespoon canola oil

Preheat waffle iron, and mist with nonstick spray, or alternatively, use a pastry brush to lightly coat with oil.

In a medium bowl, whisk together whole wheat pastry flour, all-purpose flour, crispy rice cereal, baking powder, cinnamon, and salt.

Add the banana, soymilk, and canola oil to flour mixture, whisking just until mixed. If mixture is too thick, add another tablespoon or two of soymilk as needed.

Scoop batter with a 1/3 cup measure (or smaller, depending on your waffle iron) onto the iron, and cook according to manufacturer's directions. Repeat with remaining batter and serve.

Tip: The large yield here is great for those feeding a hungry family or crowd. Not to worry though: the waffles freeze really well, perfect for popping into the toaster on harried mornings.

Orange Cornbread Waffles

Cornmeal gives these waffles a deliciously buttery flavor and a nice and crunchy texture. They are delicious topped with strawberry sauce or agave nectar and whipped Earth Balance or any vegan margarine.

MAKES ABOUT 8 BELGIAN-STYLE WAFFLES

1 cup unbleached all-purpose flour

3/4 cup yellow cornmeal

1/4 cup yellow corn flour (not cornstarch)

2 tablespoons granulated sugar

1 tablespoon baking powder

1/8 teaspoon fine sea salt

3/4 cup orange juice, preferably fresh-squeezed

3/4 cup soymilk

1 tablespoon canola oil

Preheat waffle iron, and mist with nonstick spray, or alternatively, use a pastry brush to lightly coat with oil.

In a medium bowl, whisk together flour, cornmeal, corn flour, sugar, baking powder, and salt.

In a separate bowl, mix together orange juice, soymilk, and canola oil, and add to flour mixture, stirring just until combined.

Scoop batter with a 1/3 cup measure (or smaller, depending on your waffle iron) onto the iron, and cook according to manufacturer's directions. Repeat with remaining batter and serve.

Variation: For a savory waffle, substitute 3/4 cup plain soymilk for the orange juice, and plain soymilk for the vanilla.

Tip: I use a corn flour available from Bob's Red Mill. It contains all the bran and germ from whole corn kernels, making it super-nutritious.

Remember to spoon your flour into your dry measuring cup, scraping the top with a knife or a skewer. Never scoop your flour directly from the canister, as you can wind up with much more flour than you need.

Malted Waffles

Malt has often been a traditional ingredient in diner waffles
and pancakes, but in the form of malted milk powder. For this waffle recipe, it dawned on me
that powdered barley malt extract would deliver a nice malted flavor, without the dairy.
These waffles are crisp on the outside and tender on the inside.

MAKES ABOUT 8
BELGIAN-STYLE WAFFLES

1^1/$_2$ cups all-purpose flour

^{3}/$_4$ cup quick oats

^{1}/$_2$ cup powdered barley
malt extract

4 teaspoons baking powder

Pinch sea salt

1^1/$_2$ cups soymilk or almond
milk, plus more as
needed

1 tablespoon canola oil

Preheat waffle iron, and mist with nonstick spray, or
alternatively, use a pastry brush to lightly coat with oil.

In a medium bowl, combine flour, oats, malt extract,
baking powder, and salt.

Mix together soymilk and oil, and add to flour mixture, stirring just until combined. Let batter stand for 5
minutes. If the batter gets too thick, add an additional
tablespoon or two of milk as needed.

Scoop batter with a ^{1}/$_3$ cup measure (or smaller,
depending on your waffle iron) onto the iron, and cook
according to manufacturer's directions. Repeat with
remaining batter and serve.

Powdered malt extract is a non-diastatic barley malt,
which is made from the evaporated concentrate of barley
malt (check the packaging for the correct variety). The malt
extract can also be used as a natural sweetener. Look for it
in natural foods stores and online.

Pumpkin Spice Pancakes

This is a perfect fall breakfast, rich with the flavors of pumpkin and spice. Pumpkin has loads of beta carotene too, so you can feel good about loading up your plate with these babies.

MAKES ABOUT
7 TO 8 PANCAKES

1 cup all-purpose flour

2 teaspoons baking powder

1½ tablespoons sugar

½ teaspoon ground cinnamon

¼ teaspoon ground ginger

¼ teaspoon ground nutmeg

⅛ teaspoon ground allspice

Pinch sea salt

1 cup soymilk or almond milk

½ cup canned plain pumpkin purée

½ teaspoon molasses

½ teaspoon pure vanilla extract

In a large bowl, whisk together the flour, baking powder, sugar, cinnamon, ginger, nutmeg, allspice, and salt.

In a separate bowl or measuring cup, whisk together milk, pumpkin, molasses, and vanilla. Add milk mixture to flour mixture, whisking or stirring just until mixed. There may be a few lumps left, which is okay. If batter is too thick, add a little more milk to thin, as necessary.

Heat a skillet over medium-high heat and lightly grease it. Once skillet is hot, reduce heat to medium and scoop batter by ¼ cup measure onto the skillet, spreading into 3 to 4-inch rounds. When the bottoms of the pancakes are nicely browned and bubbles begin to set around the edges, about 3 to 4 minutes, gently flip the pancakes. Continue cooking until the pancakes are set, about 3 to 4 minutes more. These pancakes tend to take a few minutes longer to cook, and get a bit darker than plain pancakes because of the pumpkin and spices, so don't worry. If necessary, turn the heat down to keep pancakes from burning. Serve pancakes hot with syrup.

Spelt Chai Pancakes

I love the nutty, whole grain flavor of spelt flour,
especially when combined with the rich and spicy flavors of chai tea. The pancakes are
delicious topped with a little Earth Balance and drizzled with maple syrup or agave nectar.

MAKES ABOUT 7 PANCAKES

$1/2$ cup boiling water

4 chai tea bags

$1/2$ cup to $2/3$ cup soymilk or almond milk, or as needed

$1/2$ cup light spelt flour

$1/2$ cup whole grain spelt flour (or use 1 cup light spelt flour)

1 tablespoon granulated sugar, preferably organic

1 tablespoon baking powder

$1/4$ teaspoon ground cinnamon

1 tablespoon canola or other light, flavorless oil

Canola oil, for cooking

Combine the hot water and tea bags in a heat-proof measuring cup. Let steep for 10 to 15 minutes. Using the back of a spoon, squeeze the extra water out of the tea bags. Discard tea bags. Add milk to the water so that you wind up with 1 cup of total liquid.

In a medium bowl, combine the light flour, whole grain flour, sugar, baking powder, and cinnamon. Add the milk mixture and oil, stirring just until combined. Do not over mix.

Heat a large skillet or griddle over medium heat and grease with a tablespoon or so of oil. Scoop the batter with $1/4$ cup measure onto hot skillet or griddle, spreading into 3 or 4-inch rounds. Cook until bubbles appear on surface, bottom is golden and edges look firm, about 2 to 3 minutes. Flip pancakes and cook until golden, about 2 to 3 minutes more. Repeat with remaining batter, adding more oil to the skillet as necessary.

Serve pancakes right away, as they are best hot.

Variation: Sprinkle fresh or frozen blueberries on top of each pancake, right after scooping batter onto hot skillet. Spelt is an ancient variety of wheat, one of the original seven grains mentioned in the Bible. It tends to be less of an allergen than wheat flour, to some sensitive individuals. It does contain gluten though, so it is not suitable for those with wheat or gluten allergies.

Whole Grain Pancake Mix

Forget that boxed pancake mix you've got in your pantry.

Here is a fantastic alternative that not only tastes better, but is much healthier, too.

2^1/$_2$ cups whole wheat pastry flour

1 cup fine or medium grind cornmeal (preferably stone-ground) or corn flour

^{1}/$_2$ cup quick-cooking oats

^{1}/$_4$ cup packed light brown sugar

2 tablespoons baking powder

^{1}/$_2$ teaspoon fine sea salt

In a large bowl, combine the whole wheat pastry flour, cornmeal, oats, brown sugar, baking powder, and salt, transfer the mixture to an airtight container. Store in the refrigerator until ready for use. Make sure to stir the pancake mixture really well before using.

To make pancakes, for every cup of mix, add 1 cup of milk (or more as needed) and 1 teaspoon of vanilla extract (plus ^{1}/$_2$ cup frozen blueberries or chopped pecans, if desired) and then cook as needed. The batter will get thicker as it stands, from the oats and cornmeal.

My Big Fat Greek Scramble

Here's a delicious start to your morning,
with all sorts of fresh vibrant Greek flavors. To really gild the breakfast lily,
serve alongside fried potatoes and some toasted whole grain bread.

SERVES 4

2 teaspoons extra-virgin
olive oil

1 small Vidalia onion,
diced (1 cup)

1 red bell pepper, seeded
and diced

$\frac{1}{2}$ cup pitted Kalamata
olives, coarsely chopped

2 large cloves garlic,
pressed

$1\frac{1}{4}$ ounces block firm
water-packed tofu,
drained and lightly
pressed

$1\frac{1}{2}$ tablespoons nutritional
yeast flakes

$1\frac{1}{2}$ teaspoons dried basil

$1\frac{1}{2}$ teaspoons dried
oregano

$1\frac{1}{2}$ teaspoons dried parsley

2 cups lightly packed fresh
baby spinach

Fine sea salt and freshly
ground black pepper,
to taste

In a large skillet, add olive oil and heat over medium high heat. Add onion, red pepper, olives, and garlic, cooking and stirring for 3 to 4 minutes, or until the vegetables have just softened. Crumble tofu into skillet and cook about 5 minutes or so, just until lightly browned. Add nutritional yeast, basil, oregano, and parsley, stirring until tofu is evenly coated. Add spinach, cooking another minute or two, just until wilted. Add salt and pepper to taste. Serve immediately.

To press the tofu for this recipe, I just give the tofu a light rinse and blot well with paper towels, lightly pressing up extra moisture with the towels. It won't be completely dry from moisture. You just want to wick away the extra. There are lots of different varieties of tofu available in the grocery store. My personal favorite for scrambles is firm or extra-firm water-packed tofu. These varieties give the scramble a bit more of a toothsome bite. If you prefer a soft texture scramble, you can use a medium-firm, water-packed tofu.

Smoky Potato Scramble

If you like fried potatoes with your scramble,

you are in luck! This dish is delish, with a garlicky savory bite.
Don't omit the smoked paprika, as that is where the magic flavor lies.

MAKES 4 SERVINGS

8 ounces small red potatoes (about 3 to 4)

2 tablespoons extra-virgin olive oil

1 small onion, diced (about 1 cup)

4 cloves garlic, pressed or minced

14 or 16-ounce container firm tofu, rinsed and blotted dry

2½ tablespoons nutritional yeast flakes

1½ teaspoons granulated onion

1 teaspoon smoked paprika

Salt and freshly ground black pepper, to taste

4 tablespoons minced fresh parsley

Fill a large pot or Dutch oven with water and bring to a boil over medium high heat. Add potatoes and cook until just tender, about 15 minutes. Drain and let sit until cool enough to handle. Dice into chunks. You can also cook the potatoes the day before, and refrigerate them overnight.

In a large skillet over medium high heat, add the oil and swirl around in the pan. Add the potatoes and onion, and cook for about 5 to 7 minutes, or until the potatoes and onions start to brown. Add the garlic, stirring well. Crumble tofu into the skillet and, stirring as needed, cook for another 5 minutes. Add the nutritional yeast, granulated onion, smoked paprika, and salt and pepper to taste, stirring well to coat. Continue cooking for another 4 minutes or so, before removing the skillet from heat. Sprinkle parsley over top, and toss to combine. Serve hot.

Smoked paprika is a richly flavored spice, with a slightly sweet undertone to it. Sometimes referred to as pimentón, smoked paprika is made in Spain from smoked, ground pimento peppers. Look for it on the spice aisle of well-stocked grocery and specialty stores or online. I've even purchased it at Costco.

Breakfast Potatoes
with Peppers and Onions

These potatoes are a weekend staple in our house,
and usually accompany a tofu scramble and fresh brewed coffee. If you want to
make them quickly in the morning, cook the potatoes the night before, and refrigerate.

MAKES 2 TO 4 SERVINGS

1 pound small red potatoes
(about 7 to 8 potatoes)

2 tablespoons extra-virgin
olive oil

1 small onion, diced (1 cup)

1 green bell pepper, diced

4 cloves garlic, pressed or
minced

2 tablespoons minced fresh
parsley

Salt and freshly ground
black pepper, to taste

Fill a large pot or Dutch oven with water and bring to a boil over medium high heat. Add the potatoes and cook until just tender, about 15 minutes. Drain and let sit until cool enough to handle. Dice the potatoes into chunks.

In a large skillet over medium high heat, add the oil and swirl around the pan. Add the potatoes in a single layer, and cook for about 10 minutes, or until golden-brown. Add the onions, peppers, and garlic and continue cooking for another 5 to 7 minutes or until the onions and peppers are soft and everything is nicely browned. I like mine pretty well done, but it's all up to your personal preference.

Sprinkle the potatoes with minced parsley and add salt and pepper to taste. Serve hot.

Variation: Serve these potatoes skillet-style. Fry them up in a cast-iron skillet, and top with sliced veggie sausages and Creamy Sage Gravy (see page 47).

Biscuits and Creamy Sage Gravy

Biscuits with gravy is one of my daughter's all-time favorite breakfasts. It makes for a hearty and filling start to the day, but is also just as yummy for dinner.

MAKES 2 TO 4 SERVINGS

- 1/4 cup all-purpose flour
- 3 tablespoons nutritional yeast flakes
- 2 cups plain unsweetened soymilk
- 1 teaspoon dried rubbed sage
- 1 teaspoon granulated onion
- 1 teaspoon fine sea salt, or to taste
- 1 teaspoon freshly ground black pepper, to taste
- 1/4 teaspoon freshly ground white pepper, or to taste
- 1 to 2 tablespoons vegan margarine
- 1 recipe Fluffy Biscuits (see page 54), sliced in half

In a large saucepan, whisk together the flour and nutritional yeast. Whisk in the soymilk until the mixture is very smooth and there are no lumps. Alternately, use an immersion blender and blend until smooth. Whisk in the sage and onion. Add salt, black pepper, and white pepper to taste.

Place the saucepan over medium heat and, whisking continuously, bring to a simmer. Whisk in the margarine. Reduce heat to medium-low, and continue whisking for 3 to 5 minutes, or until the gravy is thickened and smooth.

Remove from heat and adjust seasonings to taste. Place the biscuit halves on plates and ladle gravy over top. Serve immediately.

This gravy is fantastic on all of the usual suspects. Try it over mashed potatoes, French fries, baked potatoes, tater-tots, breakfast potatoes, seitan, open-faced savory sandwiches, and even toast.

Breakfast Benedicts Florentine

Now you can have your "eggs benny" vegan-style.

These are absolutely delicious and cholesterol-free, too. You've got to love a healthy classic!

MAKES 4 SERVINGS

6 ounces fresh baby spinach, rinsed and patted dry

2 teaspoons extra-virgin olive oil

8 homemade breakfast sausages (see page 50) or 1 package veggie ham or bacon

4 English muffins or biscuits, halved and lightly toasted

Non-hydrogenated vegan margarine, as needed

2 large tomatoes, sliced

1 batch Hollandaise Sauce (see page 160), or Garlic Dill Sauce (see page 161), kept warm

Freshly ground black pepper

Add the spinach to a large skillet, preferably nonstick, and place over medium-high heat. Cook 3 to 4 minutes or just until spinach wilts and changes color, adding water a teaspoon at a time if the spinach starts to stick. Remove from heat.

Heat a skillet over medium-high heat and add olive oil. Add sausage patties and cook 2 to 4 minutes, or until nicely browned on bottom. Flip the sausages over and cook for another 2 to 4 minutes or until browned on the other side. Remove skillet from heat.

Spread the toasted English muffins with a bit of margarine. Top each muffin half with a sausage patty, then a slice of tomato, then spinach. Repeat for the remaining English muffins. Place two muffin halves on each plate. Ladle Hollandaise sauce over each half and serve the Benedicts right away.

Variation: If you're in a rush, make a Garden Benedict. Simply top toasted English muffin halves with thick tomato slices and fresh basil, if desired, and drizzle with Garlic Dill Sauce (see page 161).

Herbed Breakfast Sausage Patties

Once you start making breakfast sausages at home,

you'll never go back to the store–bought varieties again. You can use most any kind of steamer here. Your best bet is to look for a steamer with a flat base, so that your sausages have a flat bottom. Either an electric or a large bamboo steamer set over a wok or pot with added water works really well, as do the large inexpensive metal steamers found at many Asian markets.

 MAKES ABOUT 13 PATTIES

1 cup vital wheat gluten

$1/4$ cup chickpea flour

2 tablespoons nutritional yeast flakes

1 tablespoon light brown sugar

2 teaspoons dried rubbed sage

2 teaspoons dried granulated onion

2 teaspoons dried granulated garlic

1 teaspoon dried ground rosemary

1 teaspoon dried parsley

1 teaspoon fine sea salt, or to taste

$1/2$ teaspoon dried thyme

$1/2$ teaspoon freshly ground black pepper

$1/2$ teaspoon fresh grated nutmeg

$1/2$ teaspoon red pepper flakes, or more to taste

1 tablespoon soy sauce

1 tablespoon extra-virgin olive oil

In a large bowl, whisk together the vital wheat gluten, chickpea flour, nutritional yeast flakes, brown sugar, sage, onion, garlic, rosemary, parsley, salt, thyme, black pepper, nutmeg, and red pepper flakes.

In a large measuring cup or pitcher, whisk together 1 cup water, soy sauce, and olive oil. Using a fork, gently stir into the dry ingredients. Stir just until ingredients are mixed. If the dough mixture is too dry, you can add another tablespoon of water as needed.

Scoop about 2 tablespoons ($1/8$ cup) of mixture for each patty, and shape into thin $2^{1}/_{2}$-inch rounds. An easy way to shape the sausages is to use a mini-burger press, found at many kitchen stores.

Place the patties on 6-inch squares of aluminum foil. Place the sausages on corner of foil and fold up into a little package. Don't seal the edges, just fold over. Repeat with remaining sausages. Fill the bottom of your steamer with water, if using an electric or metal one. If using a bamboo steamer, place over a wok or saucepan of simmering water. Place the sausages in the steamer in a flat layer, although they can overlap into two layers if you run out of room. You want them to be as flat as possible, to prevent the sausages from being misshapen. Steam for 30 minutes or until firm. Remove the sausages from the steamer to cool completely. Once the sausages have cooled, remove foil. Refrigerate until ready to eat, preferably overnight.

To serve, pan-fry the sausages with a little olive oil in a hot skillet over medium-high heat, until lightly browned.

Tip: The sausages may feel a bit dry on the outside. Don't worry, as they will soften and firm up considerably after chilling. You can make a big batch in advance, and freeze them for later use. There are also some great electric steamers on the market, which would work as well.

Breads

Fluffy Biscuits

If you like your biscuits tall, fluffy, and flaky, you're
going to love this recipe. They are excellent served smothered with cream gravy, topped
with sautéed spinach, tomato, and Hollandaise sauce or just slathered with vegan butter and
jam. You might want to double this recipe, because these biscuits will fly off the tray.

MAKES 6

2 cups all-purpose flour

1 tablespoon baking powder

$1/2$ teaspoon fine sea salt

4 tablespoons ($1/4$ cup) shortening, chilled

$3/4$ cup unsweetened soymilk (or other non-dairy milk)

Preheat the oven to 400°F. Line a baking sheet with
parchment paper and set aside.

In a large bowl, whisk together the flour, baking powder, and salt. Add the shortening. Using a pastry
blender, cut the shortening into the flour, until it
becomes sandy-textured and has little bits of shortening the size of small peas. Add the soymilk and stir just
until the dough comes together. It should be a little
sticky.

Place the dough on a lightly floured surface and gently pat into a mound about 1-inch thick. Using a 3-inch
round biscuit or cookie cutter (or an upside-down
glass), cut out 6 biscuits. Make sure not to twist the cutter or glass, just press straight down. The twisting
motion will prevent the biscuits from rising high.
Place the biscuits on the prepared baking sheet about
1-inch apart. Bake in the preheated oven for 15 to 20
minutes, or until golden brown.

Chipotle Scallion Double Cornbread

This cornbread might be good enough to settle the long debate between sweet and savory cornbread: it has a little spice, a little sweetness, and lots of delicious corn goodness. Add the chipotle powder to taste, as some brands can be much hotter than others.

MAKES 8 SERVINGS

- 1½ cups yellow cornmeal
- 1½ cups unbleached all-purpose flour
- 3 tablespoons granulated sugar, or to taste
- 1 tablespoon baking powder
- ½ to 1½ teaspoons ground chipotle powder, or to taste
- ½ teaspoon fine sea salt
- 1¾ cups plain, unsweetened soymilk or other non-dairy milk
- ¼ cup canola oil
- 1½ cups fresh or frozen sweet corn, thawed if frozen
- 1 cup thinly sliced scallions

Preheat the oven to 375°F. Grease a 10-inch cast-iron skillet or an 8-inch square glass baking pan with shortening.

In a large bowl, mix together the cornmeal, flour, sugar, baking powder, ground chipotle, and salt. Add the milk and oil to the flour mixture, stirring just until combined. Stir in the corn and scallions. Be careful not to over mix the batter.

Scoop the batter into the prepared pan. Bake in the preheated oven for 45 to 50 minutes, or until it's lightly brown on top, and a tester inserted into the center comes out clean. Baking times may vary slightly depending on the pan you use.

Remove the cornbread from the oven and set aside on a rack to cool. Serve warm or at room temperature.

For a fun twist with cornbread, look for different shaped pans to bake it in. Some fun pans to try are mini- and regular-sized muffin pans, cast-iron pans shaped like corn cobs, and madeleine pans (shell-shaped cookie pan).

Sweet Cornbread

I've been making this recipe for years,

and it never fails to please. In fact, serving a pot of chili without this cornbread is sacrilegious in our house. This recipe is adapted from one by cookbook author Bryanna Clark Grogan. It's a moist and tender bread, with a delicious corn flavor.

MAKES ONE 10-INCH PAN

1¹/₂ **cups medium grind yellow cornmeal**

1¹/₂ **cups unbleached all-purpose flour**

¹/₃ **cup granulated sugar**

1 **tablespoon plus 1 teaspoon baking powder**

¹/₄ **teaspoon fine sea salt**

2 **cups plain soymilk or other non-dairy milk**

¹/₄ **cup canola oil**

Preheat the oven to 400°F. Grease a 10-inch cast-iron skillet or 8-inch square glass baking pan with shortening.

In a large bowl, mix together the cornmeal, flour, sugar, baking powder, and salt. Add the soymilk and canola oil to the flour mixture, stirring just until combined. Be careful not to over mix the batter.

Scoop the batter into the prepared pan. Bake in the preheated oven for 40 to 50 minutes, or until the cornbread is lightly browned on top, and a tester inserted into the center comes out clean. Baking times may vary slightly depending on the pan you use.

Remove the cornbread from oven and set aside to cool until ready to serve.

Variation: Feel free to reduce the sugar to ¹/₄ cup or less, if you like your cornbread a little less sweet.

Although you can use a regular grind cornmeal in this recipe, I love the texture that a medium-grind cornmeal contributes to this recipe. It's a coarser stone-ground, which I think even brightens the corn flavor, too. One of my favorite brands of cornmeal comes from Bob's Red Mill.

Chocolate Hazelnut Swirl Bread

Freshly baked homemade bread hot from the oven
is one of my favorite things! Even better is sharing your homemade bread with friends
and family. What better way to show you care than to take the time to bake from scratch?
This one is doubly special, rolled up with cinnamon, sugar, chocolate, and hazelnuts.

MAKES ONE LOAF

Dough

1 package active dry yeast

1 teaspoon plus $1/3$ cup granulated sugar, divided

$1/4$ cup warm water (about 110°F)

About 3 cups all-purpose flour, plus more as needed, divided

1 cup whole wheat flour (white or regular)

3 tablespoons vital wheat gluten

2 tablespoons soymilk powder

1 teaspoon fine sea salt

2 tablespoons non-hydrogenated vegan margarine, melted

Soy creamer or soymilk, as needed

1 tablespoon coarsely granulated sugar, for topping

Filling

1 cup semisweet chocolate chips

$3/4$ cup coarsely chopped hazelnuts, toasted

$1/3$ cup light brown sugar

1 teaspoon ground cinnamon

Line a baking sheet with parchment paper or a silicone mat.

For the dough: In a small bowl, combine the yeast, 1 teaspoon sugar, and the warm water. Let stand 10 minutes, or until very foamy.

In the bowl of a stand mixer, combine $2^1/2$ cups flour, whole wheat flour, $1/3$ cup sugar, vital wheat gluten, soymilk powder, and salt, mixing until well combined. Add 1 cup water, margarine, and the reserved yeast mixture. Beat together until well mixed and the dough comes together. Switch to the dough hook and continue to beat until the dough is silky and firm. If the dough is too sticky, add the remaining flour 1 tablespoon at a time, or as needed to get a silky dough.

Place the dough in a large oiled bowl, turning the dough to lightly coat. Cover the top of the bowl with plastic wrap and set aside for about 1 to $1^1/2$ hours, or until doubled in size.

For the filling: In a small bowl, mix together the chocolate chips, hazelnuts, brown sugar, and cinnamon.

On a lightly floured surface, roll the dough out into a rectangle, approximately 13 x 17 inches, with the long edge closest to you. Sprinkle the filling over the dough, leaving a $1/4$-inch border. Starting with the edge closest to you, roll up the dough jelly-roll style into a log, pinching the edges and ends to seal. Gently grab hold of one of the ends, and tie the roll into a knot, tucking the end down through the center. Place the bread on the prepared baking sheet and cover with a towel. Let rise for *(continued on next page)*

40 minutes, or until a dent does not fill in when the dough is lightly pressed with a fingertip. Do not let the bread double in size.

Preheat the oven to 350°F.

Brush the loaf lightly with soy creamer or soymilk and sprinkle with the coarsely granulated sugar. Bake the bread in the preheated oven for about 50 minutes, or until golden-brown and loaf sounds hollow when tapped. Remove from oven and cool completely on a cooling rack.

Variation: Substitute chopped pecans or walnuts for the hazelnuts.

Cinnamon–Sugar Bread

Cinnamon bread is a definite crowd pleaser and an all–American favorite. There's nothing like those cinnamon sugar swirls and the light and fluffy texture to get people excited. Although I've left the raisins out here (to keep the peace in my house), you can certainly add them in: see the recipe variation.

MAKES 1 9 X 5-INCH LOAF

Bread

$3^1/_2$ cups all-purpose flour, plus more as needed

$^1/_4$ cup granulated sugar

$2^1/_2$ teaspoons instant yeast

1 teaspoon fine sea salt

$1^1/_4$ cups plus 2 tablespoons vanilla soymilk, lukewarm

$^1/_4$ cup canola oil

Soy creamer or soymilk

Grease a 9 x 5-inch metal loaf pan with shortening. For the dough: In the bowl of a stand mixer fitted with the paddle attachment, combine flour, sugar, instant yeast, and salt, mixing well.

Add the soymilk and oil to the flour and mix until the dough comes together. Switch to the dough hook and mix the dough for about 5 minutes, or until the dough is smooth and silky, adding more flour, 1 tablespoon at a time if dough is too sticky.

Remove the dough from bowl and shape into a ball. Place the dough into a large oiled bowl, turning the dough to lightly coat. Cover the top of the bowl with plastic wrap and set in a warm spot for about 1 to $1^1/_2$

Filling

¹/₃ cup granulated sugar

2 teaspoons ground cinnamon

Glaze

³/₄ cup confectioners' sugar

1 tablespoon vanilla soymilk

¹/₂ teaspoon pure vanilla extract

hours, or until doubled in size.

For the filling: In a small bowl, mix together the sugar and cinnamon.

On a lightly floured surface, roll the dough out into a rectangle, approximately 11 by 17-inches. Using a pastry brush, brush the entire surface lightly with water. Sprinkle the filling over the dough, leaving a ¹/₄-inch border all around. Roll up the dough tightly, jelly-roll style, beginning with the narrow side. Pinch and seal the edge and ends. Slightly tuck under the ends and place the sealed edge down into the prepared pan. Cover with a towel, and let rise for 35 to 45 minutes, or until the bread has risen about 1 to 1¹/₂ inches above the rim of the pan.

Preheat the oven to 350°F.

Brush the bread lightly with soy creamer or milk. Bake the bread in the preheated oven for about 45 to 50 minutes, or until golden brown and loaf sounds hollow when tapped, and an instant-read thermometer inserted into the center registers 190°F. If the bread appears to be browning too quickly, tent it with aluminum foil. Remove bread from the pan and cool completely on a cooling rack.

For the glaze: In a small bowl, whisk together the confectioners' sugar, soymilk, and vanilla until smooth. The glaze will be fairly thick, but if it's too thick to spread or drizzle, add another teaspoon of soymilk as needed to thin.

Spread or drizzle the glaze over the cooled loaf. Let the loaf sit for about 30 minutes, or until the glaze is firm.

Variation: For cinnamon–raisin bread, sprinkle ¹/₂ cup raisins over cinnamon sugar before rolling.

English Muffins

After realizing that I could not find a single brand of
vegan English muffins at the grocery store, I set about to bake them from scratch. After
some experimenting, I liked this recipe best. It's adapted from a recipe by Alton Brown.

MAKES 8 TO 10 MUFFINS

3 tablespoons powdered soymilk

2 tablespoons granulated sugar

1 teaspoon fine sea salt, divided

2 teaspoons instant yeast

1 cup unbleached all-purpose flour

1 cup white whole wheat flour (substitute whole wheat flour)

2 tablespoons non-hydrogenated vegan margarine, melted

1$\frac{1}{3}$ cups warm water (about 110°F)

1 teaspoon baking soda

1 tablespoon cider vinegar

Shortening or oil for greasing metal rings and pan

In a bowl, combine the powdered soymilk, sugar, $\frac{1}{2}$ teaspoon salt, yeast, all-purpose flour, and wheat flour, mixing well.

In a bowl or measuring cup, mix margarine and warm water, stirring until shortening is melted. Add water mixture to flour mixture and beat thoroughly with a spoon. Cover the bowl with plastic wrap and let it rest in a warm spot for 1 hour.

Preheat a lightly greased cast-iron skillet or griddle over medium-low heat. Lightly greased 3- to 3$\frac{3}{4}$-inch metal English muffin rings (see note.)

Add the remaining $\frac{1}{2}$ teaspoon salt and baking soda to the dough, mixing thoroughly. Stir in the cider vinegar until mixed.

When the griddle or skillet is up to heat, place well-greased rings on the griddle or skillet. Sprinkle a little cornmeal inside the ring. Scoop enough dough to fill up ring mold halfway and place into the ring. Sprinkle the top lightly with cornmeal. Cook for about 10 minutes or until it looks fairly cooked through and the bottom and sides are nicely browned. Flip rings using tongs. Cook for another 5 to 6 minutes or until golden brown. Place on a cooling rack, remove rings and cool. Split with a fork and serve.

A cast–iron drop biscuit pan works beautifully for making the English muffins (without the metal rings). Alternately, you can use empty 8–ounce pineapple cans, with both the tops and bottom removed. Look for metal muffin rings in cooking stores or online.

Double Cornbread Buns

This fantastic recipe is courtesy of baker extraordinaire
Melisser Elliott. The buns are soft and tender, rich with the buttery flavor of corn and are perfect stuffed
with a veggie burger or sloppy Joe filling. For extra help with wintertime bread-baking, see page 14.

MAKES 6 BUNS

2 cups unbleached all-purpose flour, plus more as needed

³/₄ cup cornmeal

2 teaspoons instant yeast

1 teaspoon fine sea salt

²/₃ cup warm water (about 110°F)

2 tablespoons non-hydrogenated vegan margarine, melted

2 tablespoons agave nectar

¹/₂ cup corn, fresh or frozen and defrosted

Cornmeal, as needed for sprinkling

Line a baking sheet with parchment paper or a silicone mat, and sprinkle lightly with cornmeal.

In the bowl of a stand mixer, combine the flour, cornmeal, instant yeast, and salt, beating until combined. Add the warm water, melted margarine, agave nectar, and corn, beating on low speed until combined. Switch to the dough hook and continue beating until you have a soft and slightly sticky dough that pulls away from the sides of bowl. If the dough is too sticky, add additional flour, a teaspoon at a time, until you have a soft and silky dough. Let the mixer knead the dough for another minute or two. Place the dough in a large oiled bowl, turning the dough to lightly coat. Cover the top of the bowl with plastic wrap. Place the bowl in a warm spot and let sit about 1 hour, or until doubled in size.

Preheat the oven to 375°F.

Turn the dough out onto a lightly floured work surface and divide the dough into 6 pieces. Shape the pieces into balls and place on the prepared baking sheet. Lightly flatten the balls into 3¹/₂-inch discs.

Cover the buns with a slightly damp kitchen towel and let them rise until puffed, about 30 to 40 minutes. Place buns in the preheated oven and bake for 20 to 25 minutes, or until golden on top, browned on the bottom and sound hollow when tapped on the base.

Let the buns cool completely before slicing.

Variation: You can substitute oil for the margarine, although it won't be as buttery-tasting.

Old-Fashioned Hamburger Buns

Although burger buns can be purchased easily

at your local market, it's super-simple to make them from scratch. This recipe is pretty quick and easy to make, and one that you'll want to use often.

MAKES ABOUT 6 BUNS

3 cups unbleached all-purpose flour, plus more as needed

2 tablespoons granulated sugar

2$\frac{1}{2}$ teaspoons instant yeast

1 teaspoon fine sea salt

1 cup plain soymilk, lukewarm

3 tablespoons olive oil or canola oil

Plain soymilk, for brushing

Sesame seeds

Preheat the oven to 400°F. Line a large baking sheet with parchment paper or a silicone mat.

In the bowl of a stand mixer, combine the flour, sugar, instant yeast, and salt, mixing well.

Add the soymilk and the oil to the flour mixture and beat until the dough comes together. Switch to the dough hook and mix the dough for about 5 minutes, or until the dough is smooth and silky, adding more flour, 1 tablespoon at a time if dough is too sticky.

Remove the dough from bowl and shape into a log. Cover with a slightly damp towel and let sit for 15 minutes, to give the gluten a chance to relax. Divide the dough into 6 pieces, and form each piece into a ball. For hamburger buns, flatten the balls into 3$\frac{1}{2}$-inch disks. Place on the prepared baking sheet about 2 inches apart. Let rise for 20 minutes. If you want the buns to be softer, place them closer together (about $\frac{1}{2}$ inch apart), so that they will be touching when they rise.

Lightly brush the tops of the buns with plain soymilk and sprinkle with sesame seeds. Bake the buns for about 15 minutes, or until golden brown. The internal temperature should register 190°F on an instant-read thermometer. Let the buns cool on the baking sheet for 5 minutes, before removing to a rack to cool completely.

When ready to serve, slice the buns in half horizontally and fill with veggie burgers.

Tip: To make hot dog buns, roll the balls into cylinders, 4$\frac{1}{2}$ inches in length. Flatten the cylinders slightly. For slider buns, simply make 12 buns instead of 6.

Rosemary Sandwich Rolls

These rolls are a tasty way to liven up your sandwiches, with the zesty bite of garlic and rosemary. The dough can be made the day before and refrigerated after the first rise. One word of caution though: once you start baking your own rolls, you'll never want to go back to the store–bought variety again.

3 cups unbleached all-purpose flour, plus more as needed

1 tablespoon granulated sugar

2 teaspoons instant yeast

1 teaspoon fine sea salt

1 cup warm water

1 tablespoon olive oil, plus more for the bowl and brushing on crusts

2 teaspoons finely chopped fresh rosemary

3 large cloves garlic, pressed or finely minced

1 tablespoon agave nectar

Line a large baking sheet with parchment paper or a silicone mat.

In bowl of a stand mixer fitted with the paddle attachment, combine the flour, sugar, instant yeast, and salt, mixing well.

Add water, olive oil, rosemary, garlic, and agave to the flour mixture and mix until the dough comes together. Switch to the dough hook and beat the dough for about 5 minutes, or until the dough is smooth and silky, adding more flour, 1 teaspoon at a time, if dough is too sticky.

Transfer the dough to an oiled bowl, cover with plastic wrap and let rise for about 1 hour, or until doubled in size. You can let this dough rise as long as 4 hours.

Preheat the oven to 350°F.

While the oven is preheating, shape the rolls. Divide the dough into 4 pieces. Roll each piece into a log, about 8 inches long. Place the logs on the prepared baking sheet and cover with a towel. Let rise for 20 minutes. Bake in the preheated oven for 20 to 30 minutes, or until rolls are golden and sound hollow when tapped.

Remove the tray from the oven to cool for 10 minutes. Transfer rolls to a cooling rack to cool completely before using.

Tip: The dough can also be made in a food processor.

Garlic–Dill Bread

This recipe has to be one of the very easiest loaves to make.

When time is of the essence and I want to serve a delicious loaf of bread for dinner, this is the recipe that I reach for. It's also fantastic served warm with dinner, slathered with a little vegan margarine.

MAKES ONE
9-INCH LOAF

- 3 cups unbleached all-purpose flour, plus more as needed
- 2 tablespoons baking powder
- 3 tablespoons granulated sugar
- 3/4 teaspoon fine sea salt
- 2 teaspoons dried dill or 2 tablespoons fresh dill, chopped
- 12 ounces beer, at room temperature (*see note*)
- 2 large cloves of garlic, minced or pressed

Preheat the oven to 350°F. Grease a 9 x 5-inch metal loaf pan with shortening.

In a large bowl, whisk together the flour, baking powder, sugar, salt, and dill. Slowly add the beer, stirring, just until the batter comes together into a sticky mass. Stir in the garlic.

Spread the batter in the prepared baking pan. Bake in the preheated oven for 45 to 50 minutes, or until golden brown and a tester inserted in the center comes out clean.

Remove the loaf from the oven and cool in the pan on a rack for 10 minutes. Remove the bread from the pan and cool for 10 minutes more. Serve the bread warm, with a little softened margarine or a drizzle of good olive oil.

Variation: For a whole wheat version, substitute 2 cups whole wheat flour and 1 cup unbleached all-purpose flour for the 3 cups flour.

Get creative when it comes to the beer in this recipe. I've tried it with many different styles of beer, depending on what my husband has in the fridge, and they've all worked. I tend to gravitate towards the microbrews, as they often have interesting and rich flavors. The different beers will contribute different flavors to the bread; try stout, hefeweizen, or even pale ale.

Look for dry instant yeast. It's a little different than active dry yeast and worth finding in grocery stores, online, or in the big box "club" stores. I've even found it in local stores that sell to the restaurant trade. This is where I often find 1-pound packages for a couple of dollars. Look for the SAF or Fleischmann brands. It's best to store all of your dry yeast in the freezer. If you buy it in bulk, like I do, keep the yeast in an airtight container in the freezer. This will keep your yeast fresher for a longer period of time.

Soups, Salads, & Sides

Old-Fashioned Tomato Soup

There's nothing like a bowl of creamy tomato soup,
especially alongside a grilled cheese sandwich or burger. The puréed cashews in this
recipe lend a silky and creamy texture. This soup is truly comfort food.

MAKES 4 SERVINGS

⅓ cup raw cashews

4 large cloves garlic

1 (28-ounce) can organic
  diced tomatoes

2 teaspoons or 1 small
  cube vegetarian bouillon
  powder (preferably
  chicken style)

½ teaspoon dried marjoram

½ teaspoon dried basil

12 large fresh basil leaves,
  plus additional for
  garnish

Fine sea salt or coarse salt,
  to taste

Freshly ground black
  pepper, to taste

In jar of a blender or bowl of a food processor, combine
2 cups of water and the cashews. Let cashews soak for
10 minutes. Add the garlic, tomatoes, bouillon powder,
marjoram, and dried basil to blender, blending until
completely smooth. Depending on the strength of your
blender, this may take a few minutes. Add the basil
leaves and pulse or lightly blend just until the basil is
chopped into little small pieces, not puréed. Pour the
tomato mixture into a large saucepan.

Heat the soup just until it starts to come to a simmer.
Remove from heat. Season with salt and pepper to
taste and serve.

Serve soup with a sprinkle of basil slivers, if desired.

Home-Style Veggie Noodle Soup

This deli-style noodle soup is one of my very favorites. It's perfect when it's cold outside or you're under the weather and need something warm and comforting. I have fed this soup to many people over the years, and none can believe that it doesn't contain meat. This recipe is mother-approved.

MAKES 6 TO 8 SERVINGS

2 cups sliced carrots

2 cups chopped celery

$1/2$ small onion, chopped

$1/3$ cup nutritional yeast flakes

2 tablespoons vegetarian chicken-style bouillon powder

2 teaspoons granulated onion or onion powder

1 teaspoon granulated garlic or garlic powder

$1/2$ teaspoon fine sea salt, or to taste

3 ounces dried spaghetti or linguine noodles, broken into pieces

Dash of white and black pepper, to taste

Dried or fresh chopped dill for garnish (optional)

In a large pot, combine 3 quarts water, carrots, celery, onion, nutritional yeast, bouillon powder, granulated onion, granulated garlic, salt, and the noodles. Bring soup to a simmer over medium high heat, reduce heat to medium low, and simmer for 20 to 40 minutes, stirring occasionally, until the noodles are cooked and the vegetables are tender.

Add the white and black pepper to taste, garnish with dill and serve.

Variation: To add a little protein to this soup, feel free to sprinkle in $1/4$ to $1/2$ cup of TSP or TVP granules (or crumbled Soy Curls) into the hot broth (or however much you like, really).

Vegetarian chicken-style broth granules or powder is available in many health food stores in the bulk bin section or with the other bouillon cubes and powders. If you can find it, I particularly like the flavor of the Harvest 2000 brand in this recipe. I have seen it both in grocery stores and online.

Quick and Hearty Chili

Everyone needs a great, quick chili recipe in their repertoire. This is that recipe. It tastes rich and flavorful, as if it has been simmering on the stovetop for hours. In reality, it only takes 15 minutes to simmer, and you have a perfect pot of chili, ready to grace your table with some homemade cornbread. This recipe was inspired by Bryanna Clark Grogan's award-winning chili recipe.

MAKES 4 SERVINGS

1 tablespoon olive oil

$^1/_2$ onion, chopped

3 cloves garlic, minced or pressed

$^1/_2$ bell pepper, any color, finely chopped

2 (15.5 ounces) cans kidney or pinto beans, rinsed and drained

1 (15.5 ounces) can tomato purée or 1 (15.5 ounces) can diced tomatoes, puréed

1 tablespoon soy sauce

1 tablespoon plus $^1/_2$ teaspoon regular chili powder

1 tablespoon dark cocoa powder

$1^1/_4$ teaspoons ground cumin

1 teaspoon dried oregano

1 teaspoon fine sea salt

$^1/_2$ teaspoon smoked paprika

$^1/_2$ cup TVP or TSP granules

In a large saucepan, add olive oil and heat over medium-high heat. Add the onions and garlic, and cook, stirring occasionally, until the onions are starting to soften and turn golden, about 5 to 6 minutes. Add the bell pepper and cook, stirring, for another 3 minutes.

Add $1^1/_2$ cups of water, and reduce the heat to medium-low. Add the beans, puréed tomato, soy sauce, chili powder, cocoa, cumin, oregano, salt, and paprika, stirring well. Bring the mixture to a simmer. Stir in the TSP, and reduce the heat to low. Add more water as needed.

Let the chili simmer over low heat for 15 minutes. Adjust the seasonings to taste and serve.

Diner House Salad

I couldn't write a diner book without including a house salad
recipe, now could I? This house salad is a more modern and healthful version, and is
open to a lot of different additions, so think of it as a salad blueprint.

MAKES 4 SERVINGS

8 cups mixed mesclun salad
mix, chopped romaine
hearts or baby spinach,
preferably organic

1/2 small carrot, peeled
and shredded

1 sweet yellow onion,
thinly sliced

2 tablespoons sunflower
seeds

2 tablespoons hemp seeds

Diner House Dressing
(see page 165)

Sea salt and freshly ground
black pepper, to taste

In a large bowl, combine the lettuce, carrot, onion, sunflower seeds, and hemp seeds. Drizzle with the dressing and toss well. Add salt and freshly ground pepper,
tossing well. Serve the salad right away.

Variation: Use all sunflower seeds for the hemp seeds, or
vice versa. Croutons are delicious here, too. You can also
omit the carrot and onion and add thinly sliced red apple
and dried cranberries or golden raisins. Other options are
to substitute nuts (such as toasted chopped hazelnuts,
pecans, walnuts, or almonds) for the seeds. The options are
endless!

Smoky Spinach and Tomato Salad

My son calls this the BLT salad, because it is filled
with all of the great flavors of the classic sandwich. The Smoky Strips and Creamy
Tomato Dressing are what make this salad a home run! Feel free to double the recipe.

SERVES 4 AS A SIDE
OR 2 AS A MAIN COURSE

**5 ounces baby spinach,
preferably organic**

**2 large Roma tomatoes or
large beefsteak tomato,
diced into large pieces**

Smoky Curls (see page 76)

**Creamy Tomato Dressing
(see page 164)**

**Freshly ground black
pepper, to taste**

In a large bowl, combine the spinach, tomatoes, and
Smoky Curls. Drizzle with ¾ of the Creamy Tomato
Dressing and freshly ground pepper, tossing well. Serve
right away with the remaining dressing on the side.

Tip: This salad is also equally delicious with crispy croutons.

Variation: Swap the Creamy Tomato Dressing for the
Diner House Dressing for a different, but totally delicious
salad.

Sandwich Slaw

I call this sandwich slaw because it's the ideal partner
to a Q Sandwich (page 96). Coleslaw gets better as it sits, which gives
you time to make the rest of the sandwiches.

(page 96)

MAKES 4 SANDWICH-
SIZE SERVINGS OR
2 SIDE SALADS

4 cups packed thinly shredded green cabbage

1/4 cup vegan mayonnaise

1 tablespoon cider vinegar

1/2 teaspoon agave nectar,
or to taste

1/4 teaspoon celery seed

2 cloves garlic, pressed or
finely minced

Salt and freshly ground
black or white pepper,
to taste

In a large bowl, combine the cabbage, mayonnaise, cider vinegar, agave, celery seed, and garlic, tossing well. Add salt and pepper to taste.

Let the slaw sit for 15 minutes so that flavors have a chance to meld and cabbage softens slightly. Serve slaw on Q sandwiches, or as a side salad.

Variation: For a spicy, kicky slaw, omit the celery seed and add Creole or Old Bay Seasoning to taste.

For years I thought that I didn't like coleslaw, as it seemed to be a soggy salad served in small cups alongside sandwiches and burgers. Boy was I wrong. Homemade slaw need not resemble the mass-produced versions, but instead can be a flavorful salad with some crunch and lots of flavor.

Smoky Curls

Here is my version of veggie bacon, with a smoky, salty, and slightly sweet flavor. I have found myself making these gems over and over again, whether I put them into recipes, or just munch them out of hand.

2 cups boiling water

3 tablespoons soy sauce, divided

2 tablespoons liquid smoke, divided

4 ounces dry Soy Curls

1/4 teaspoon fine sea salt, optional

1/4 teaspoon freshly ground pepper, or to taste

2 teaspoons olive oil, or more as needed

1 tablespoon agave nectar, any variety

In a medium bowl, combine boiling water, 2 tablespoons soy sauce, and 1 tablespoon liquid smoke. Add the Soy Curls and stir until well mixed. Set aside for 10 minutes, or until the Soy Curls are soft. Transfer them to a colander and drain well, pressing on the Soy Curls to remove the excess liquid. Remove any excess liquid from the bowl. Return the drained Soy Curls to the bowl, and stir in the remaining tablespoon of liquid smoke, the remaining tablespoon of soy sauce, salt, and the pepper. Stir until evenly coated.

Preheat a large cast-iron skillet over medium-high heat. Add the oil, coating the bottom of the pan. Add the Soy Curls and cook, stirring every few minutes, for 5 to 10 minutes, until the Soy Curls are nicely browned. If necessary, reduce the heat to keep them from burning. Drizzle the agave over the curls, tossing them well with a fork, until they are all lightly coated. Cook another minute or two, until they are slightly caramelized, and remove from the heat. Enjoy hot or cool.

Tip: You can make these crispy or soft, depending on your preferences. You can also add a little more oil when you are cooking them, if needed or if you want them to be a little richer and crispier.

For a truly stellar sandwich, try these Smoky Curls with lettuce and tomato, on lightly toasted sourdough or rustic bread (with a little smear of vegan mayo!).

You can purchase Soy Curls online (see Resources, page 183). They are a dry product, and will rehydrate easily in hot liquid. I love them, and always have a bag on hand in my freezer.

Creamy Horseradish Potato Salad

My husband Jay is the brains behind this recipe,
and let me just say that it's fantastic! This is a signature dish, one that
he's been making for many years. The horseradish flavor actually mellows
as it sits, so if you love horseradish like I do, add extra to taste.

MAKES 4 SERVINGS

2 pounds small red potatoes, peeled

¹/₃ cup plain unsweetened soymilk

¹/₂ cup vegan mayonnaise, plus more as needed

2 to 3 tablespoons prepared horseradish, or more as needed

¹/₂ teaspoon fine sea salt, or to taste

Freshly ground pepper, to taste

In a large pot of lightly salted boiling water, add potatoes and cook until just tender, about 15 to 20 minutes. Drain and let sit until cool enough to handle. Dice into large chunks.

In a large bowl, stir together the soymilk, mayonnaise, horseradish, and salt. Add the diced potatoes to the bowl and toss to coat with the mayonnaise mixture. Give the potato salad a few good stirs, as it helps the salad become thick and creamy. Season to taste with salt and pepper.

Serve the potato salad right away, or refrigerate until ready to serve. If you're not serving the salad right away, you may need to add a little more mayo to keep it creamy. The potatoes have a way of soaking it all up.

One of my recipe testers said that when she first made this salad, it was hard for her to not add extra stuff into it. But, she said, after tasting the salad, she was really happy that she left it alone. I often add extra goodies to recipes too (a pinch more of this, and a sprinkle of that), but this is truly one salad that stands out in its simplicity. Good job, Jay!

Garlic–Dill Potato Salad

Potato salad is usually one of the first dishes to disappear at a potluck. This variation of the much-loved salad pairs garlic and fresh dill, one of my favorite combinations. It's really fresh-tasting, which is a nice change from run-of-the-mill deli salad.

MAKES 4 SERVINGS

2 pounds small red potatoes

1 cup Garlic Mayo (see page 172)

1/4 cup minced fresh dill

2 large cloves garlic, pressed or finely minced

1 teaspoon fine sea salt

Freshly ground pepper, to taste

In a large pot of lightly salted boiling water, add potatoes and cook until just tender, about 15 to 20 minutes. Drain and let sit until cool enough to handle. Dice into large chunks.

In a large bowl, stir together the mayonnaise, fresh dill, garlic, salt, and pepper. Add the diced potatoes to the bowl and toss to coat with the mayonnaise mixture. Give the potato salad a few good stirs, as it helps the salad become thick and creamy. Season to taste with salt and pepper.

Serve the potato salad right away, or refrigerate until ready to serve.

All-American Beer-Battered Onion Rings

When I want to really make my kids happy,

the quickest way to their hearts are home-fried onion rings. There's just something
about crispy hot onion rings dipped in ketchup that brings out the kid in all of us.

MAKES 4 SERVINGS

4 to 6 cups vegetable oil for frying (or as needed)

1 cup unbleached all-purpose flour

1 teaspoon granulated garlic or garlic powder

¾ teaspoon fine sea salt

½ teaspoon granulated onion or onion powder

¼ teaspoon paprika

¼ teaspoon freshly ground pepper

Dash or two of cayenne pepper

1 cup beer (preferably pale ale), room temperature

1 tablespoon fresh minced parsley

1 very large sweet white or yellow onion

4 to 6 cups vegetable oil for frying (or as needed)

Fill a large, deep pot or Dutch oven with most of the oil, making sure that the oil is at least 4 inches deep and heat the oil to 365°F.

In a large bowl, whisk together the flour, garlic, salt, onion, paprika, black pepper, and cayenne. Slowly add the beer, whisking until smooth. Add the parsley, whisking until mixed. Let the batter sit for 15 minutes. Prepare a plate covered with paper towels for draining the cooked onion rings.

Dredge the onion slices in the batter until evenly coated. Let any excess batter drip off, although you want as much of the batter as possible to stay on the onion. Use a candy thermometer to read the heat of the oil. You can also test if the oil is ready by dredging a piece of bread in the batter and dipping it in the oil. If it sizzles immediately and begins to brown, the oil's ready, if not, continue to heat the oil. If the bread burns, take the pan off the heat and let the oil cool down a bit.

Working in batches, use tongs to place them one by one in the hot oil. Do not crowd or overlap. Fry in the hot oil until golden brown and tender, turning once or twice as necessary, about 1 to 2 minutes on each side. Remove from the oil and drain on paper towels. Continue with the remaining onion rings. The oil temperature will fluctuate, cooling down slightly as you add new batches , and heating up as it sits on the heat, so carefully monitor the oil between batches. Add more oil to maintain at least 4 inches in the pot, making sure to get it back up to temperature betwen batches. Season with additional salt and pepper, and serve hot.

Crispy Chickpea Onion Rings

You can never have too many onion ring recipes,

as each one can offer something a little different. These delicious smoky-
flavored onion rings are dipped in a chickpea batter, which gives them a
crisp exterior and a sweet, soft middle. They are gluten-free, too.

MAKES 4 SERVINGS

4 to 6 cups vegetable oil
for frying (or as needed)

1 cup chickpea flour

1¼ teaspoons garlic salt

¾ teaspoon smoked
paprika

¼ teaspoon freshly ground
pepper, or more to taste

¾ cup plus 2 tablespoons
sparkling water

1 very large red onion,
preferably sweet

4 to 6 cups vegetable oil
for frying (or as needed)

In a large, deep pot or Dutch oven, pour enough oil to completely submerge the onion rings, about 3 to 4 inches in a medium-sized pot, and heat to 365°F.

In a large bowl, whisk together the chickpea flour, garlic salt, smoked paprika, and black pepper. Slowly add the sparkling water, whisking just until smooth. Let the batter sit for 15 minutes. If the batter is too thick, you can add another drop or two of sparkling water. The batter should be the consistency of a pancake batter (not too thin or too thick).

Dredge the onion slices in the batter, until evenly coated. Let any excess batter drip off, although you want as much of the batter as possible to stay on the onion. Use a candy thermometer to read the temperature of the oil. You can also test if the oil is ready by dredging a piece of bread in the batter and dipping it in the oil. If it sizzles immediately and begins to brown, the oil's ready, if not, continue to heat the oil. If the bread burns, take the pan off the heat and let the oil cool down a bit.

Working in batches, use tongs to place them one by one in the hot oil. Do not crowd or overlap the onions. Fry in the hot oil until golden brown and tender, turning once or twice as necessary, about 1 to 2 minutes or each side. Remove from the oil and drain on paper towels. Continue with the remaining onion rings. The oil temperature will fluctuate, cooling down slightly as you add new batches of onion rings to the hot oil, and heating up as it sits on the heat, so carefully monitor the oil between batches. If the oil level looks like it's getting low, you can add more oil as necessary so that you have at least 4 inches of oil in the pot, making sure to get it back up to temperature between batches. Season with additional garlic salt, if desired, and serve hot.

Chickpea flour is the same as garbanzo bean flour. It can also be found labeled as besan flour in Indian grocery stores as well. Chickpea flour is gluten-free, making it a perfect choice for those who avoid gluten in their diet. The flour is rich in protein, and has a rich, slightly sweet flavor.

Vampire Fries

I can't imagine ordering at a diner without a side of fries. But these garlicky potatoes take fries to a whole new level. This recipe is a little tip of the hat to my French roots, American-style.

MAKES 4 SERVINGS

4 to 6 cups vegetable oil, for frying (or as needed)

4 large Idaho or russet baking potatoes (about 2 pounds), peeled, rinsed, and patted dry and cut into fries $1/4$ inches wide

$1/2$ cup fresh Italian parsley

3 to 4 large cloves garlic

Fine sea salt

Fill a large, deep pot or Dutch oven with at least 4 inches of oil. Heat the oil to 365°F.

Use a candy thermometer to read the temperature of the oil. You can also test if the oil is ready by dipping a piece of bread in the oil. If the bread sizzles immediately and begins to brown, the oil's ready, if not, continue to heat the oil. If the bread burns, take the pan off the heat and let the oil cool down a bit.

Working in batches, use tongs to place the fries in the hot oil. Fry the potatoes in small batches until lightly golden, about 4 to 5 minutes per batch. You don't really want to brown them, as they will be fried a second time. Remove from the oil and drain on paper towels. Let the fries sit for 10 minutes. The oil temperature will fluctuate, cooling down slightly as you add fries to the hot oil, and heating up as it sits on the heat, so carefully monitor the oil between batches. Add more oil as necessary to maintain at least 4 inches of oil in the pot, making sure to get it back up to temperature.

While the potatoes are frying, combine the parsley and garlic in a food processor and whiz until both are finely minced and fragrant. You don't want it to become a paste, just very finely minced. Set aside.

Raise the heat of the oil to 375°F. Fry the potatoes a second time in batches, being careful not to overcrowd them, until they are golden brown and crisp, about 2 minutes. Drain on fresh paper towels. Sprinkle with salt and parsley-garlic mixture and serve right away.

Sweetheart Fries

These yam fries are utterly addictive, and the perfect side dish
for a homemade veggie burger. They're a little sweet (like your sweetheart), a little smoky and a
little salty. Yams are full of beta-carotene, so they are as good for you as they are delicious. Oven
fries won't get as crispy as deep-fried versions, so don't fret if they seem soft during baking.

SERVES 2
HUNGRY PEOPLE

2 large yams

1 tablespoon olive oil

**1 tablespoon granulated
sugar**

Kosher salt or fine sea salt

**Freshly ground black
pepper**

Smoked paprika, to taste

Preheat the oven to 425°F. Line 1 to 2 baking sheets with parchment paper.

Using a sharp knife or a mandoline, slice the yams into thin, French fry-size slices.

In a large bowl, combine the yam slices, olive oil, sugar, a few pinches of salt, and pepper, tossing well to coat. Transfer the yams to the prepared baking sheet in a thin layer. If necessary, bake the yams fries on two separate baking sheets to avoid overlapping. Sprinkle the tops of the fries with smoked paprika to taste. Bake the fries until the edges are crisp and yams are cooked through, about 30 to 45 minutes, checking and stirring frequently to brown on all sides. You may need to rotate the baking sheet halfway through to prevent the fries from baking unevenly. Sprinkle with additional salt and smoked paprika, and serve immediately.

Tip: These fries are delicious dipped in homemade Creamy Ranch Dressing (see page 163).

Garlic Mashers

I am crazy for mashed potatoes! This recipe does
not dissapoint, and will have you craving them on a regular basis. I like to think of these as
diner potatoes, as they have a nice rustic flair being hand-smashed and with the skins still on.

MAKES 4 SERVINGS

**3 pounds small red
potatoes**

**About 1 cup plain unsweet-
ened soymilk, or as
needed**

**2 tablespoons non-hydro-
genated vegan margarine,
melted, or more to taste**

**¼ cup nutritional yeast
flakes**

**1 teaspoon fine sea salt, or
more to taste**

**½ teaspoon finely ground
white pepper**

**Freshly ground black pep-
per, to taste**

In a large pot of lightly salted boiling water, add potatoes
and cook until tender, about 20 to 25 minutes. Drain and
let sit for 10 minutes, or until still warm but cool enough
to handle. Transfer the potatoes to a large bowl.

Heat the soymilk until steaming hot, either in a small
saucepan on the stovetop or in the microwave.

Using a potato masher, mash the potatoes well. It's
okay if there are still some little chunks in them. Add
half of the hot milk, the melted margarine, nutritional
yeast flakes, salt, and white pepper, mixing well. At this
point, you can continue mixing by hand, or can use an
electric hand mixer with beater blades. Add more hot
milk as necessary, until the potatoes are soft and fluffy.
Add freshly ground pepper to taste. Adjust seasonings
and serve right away while hot.

Variation: Substitute plain soy creamer for the soymilk, if
you are craving something richer. You can also increase the
margarine to 4 tablespoons, if desired. For a garlic and
parsley variation, add 2 large cloves garlic finely minced or
pressed, plus ¼ cup minced fresh parsley when you're
adding the other seasonings.

This recipe is open to all kinds of customizations. Sometimes I will reduce the milk by ½ cup or so and stir some hot
gravy right into the mix. Delicious! You can also substitute
roasted garlic for the fresh (4 to 8 cloves). Feel free to also
substitute Yukon Gold potatoes for a nice buttery flavor, or
large brown russet potatoes. You can also peel the potatoes,
and use a potato ricer, which will give you a beautiful
silky texture.

Garlic–Roasted Brussels Sprouts

These roasted sprouts are deliciously addictive,
and an especially easy recipe to make. I have watched this recipe turn Brussels sprouts
haters into lovers with a single bite. These are delicious served as a fall or winter side dish.

MAKES 4 SERVINGS

1 pound small fresh Brussels
sprouts, rinsed

2 tablespoons extra-virgin
olive oil

Freshly ground black
pepper, to taste

A couple of pinches of
kosher or coarse sea salt

2 to 3 large cloves garlic,
pressed

Preheat the oven to 400°F. Line a baking sheet with parchment paper.

In a medium bowl, toss together the Brussels sprouts, olive oil, pepper, and salt, until the sprouts are well coated.

Spread the sprouts into an even layer on the prepared baking sheet. Place them in the preheated oven and bake for 20 to 25 minutes, or until the sprouts are just tender and crispy on the outside. You may need to give the sprouts a stir or two during baking, so that they roast evenly.

Carefully scoop the hot roasted sprouts into a bowl. Sprinkle fresh garlic into the bowl. Add additional salt to taste, and a few grinds of black pepper. Toss well and serve.

Diner–Style Dressing

Being from the west coast, we refer to dressing as "stuffing," but calling it dressing seems more appropriate here. This dish is full of flavor, with toasted bread cubes, fresh sage, onions, celery, and dried cranberries. The dressing is delicious for Thanksgiving, but just as good at home any time of the year topped with homemade gravy.

1^1/$_2$ cups vegetable stock or 1^1/$_2$ cups very hot water plus 1 to 2 tablespoons vegetarian chicken-style bouillon powder or cubes, or to taste (this will depend on the saltiness of the bouillon you're using), plus more as necessary

7 cups lightly packed cubed French bread (1 baguette)

1 tablespoon olive oil

4 small stalks celery, thinly sliced

1 small yellow onion, finely chopped

2 tablespoons nutritional yeast flakes

2 teaspoons fresh sage leaves, minced, or 1 teaspoon dried

^{1}/$_2$ teaspoon dried marjoram

Freshly ground white and black pepper, to taste

Fine sea salt to taste

^{1}/$_2$ cup dried cranberries

2 tablespoons non-hydrogenated vegan margarine, melted

Preheat oven to 375°F. Lightly grease a 2-quart casserole dish.

In a measuring cup, mix together the hot water and bouillon powder. In a large bowl, drizzle the hot bouillon over the bread cubes, tossing until the bread cubes are well coated. Set aside.

In a large skillet over medium-high heat, add the oil and swirl to coat the bottom of the pan. Add the celery and onion and cook, stirring as needed, until tender, about 10 to 15 minutes. If the onion mixture is starting to stick and burn, add a couple of tablespoons of water, as needed.

Add the sautéed onion mixture to the bread cubes, along with the nutritional yeast flakes, sage, and marjoram. Add the ground white and black pepper to taste. Adjust seasonings, adding salt to taste if necessary. Stir in the cranberries.

Transfer the dressing mixture to the greased baking dish, cover with a lid or foil and bake in the preheated oven for 15 minutes. Uncover the dressing, drizzle with the melted margarine and return to the oven, uncovered. Bake the dressing for 30 to 40 minutes, or until the dressing is lightly browned and crispy on top. Serve hot.

Main Courses

Rockin' Reubens

This sandwich is one of the best sellers at our food cart,

Native Bowl! It has its own cult following with devoted meat–eaters swooning alongside vegans.

MAKES 4 SANDWICHES

8 slices rye or sourdough bread

About $\frac{1}{4}$ cup non-hydrogenated vegan margarine, softened

1 tablespoon olive oil

About 14 ounces very thinly sliced Pastrami-Style Seitan Roast (see page 115)

Very Secret Sauce, as needed (see page 166)

About 1 cup shredded vegan white cheese or 4 slices soy cheese (optional)

Prepared sauerkraut, as needed

Spread a little margarine on the outside of each slice of bread. Place the bread slices in pairs on your work-space, buttered side down.

Heat a large griddle or skillet over medium-high heat. Add the oil and swirl to coat. Add the seitan and sauté briefly, so that it gets warm and just a touch toasty. Remove the seitan from the skillet and transfer to a plate.

Spread the insides of each slice of bread with about 1 to 2 tablespoons of the Very Secret Sauce, or to your liking. Place $\frac{1}{4}$ of the warm seitan on top of each of 4 bread slices. Sprinkle about $\frac{1}{4}$ cup cheese (or less, depending on your preference) over the seitan. Spoon sauerkraut over the cheese in an even layer, to your taste. Drizzle another 1 to 2 tablespoons of the Very Secret Sauce over the sauerkraut, and top with the remaining 4 slices of bread, buttered side up.

Place sandwiches onto the griddle, buttered side down, in batches if necessary. Cook until the bottoms are golden and lightly toasty. Carefully flip sandwiches over to toast the other side. If you have a smaller cast-iron skillet, place it over the sandwiches to press them. Continue cooking until the bread is lightly toasted. Serve hot sandwiches right away.

Very Sloppy Joes

I like to think of this recipe as a one–skillet meal.

It can feed a hungry family or crowd pretty quickly, which is not an easy thing to do for a busy weeknight meal. Feel free to customize the recipe further to fit your individual tastes.

MAKES 4 SANDWICHES

1 cup dried TVP or TSP granules

1 cup boiling water, or more or less as needed

1 tablespoon olive oil, plus more as needed

1 small onion, chopped

4 cloves garlic, minced or pressed

10 ounces cremini, baby bellas, or brown button mushrooms, sliced

3/4 teaspoon smoked paprika

1/2 teaspoon ground cumin

1/2 teaspoon dried garlic or garlic powder

1 (15-ounce) can tomato sauce

2 tablespoons Bragg Liquid Aminos or soy sauce

1/2 teaspoon agave nectar

1/2 teaspoon liquid smoke

Kosher salt and freshly ground black pepper

Dash of cayenne pepper, or to taste

In a medium bowl mix together the TVP and boiling water and cover with a piece of aluminum foil or plastic wrap. Set aside for 10 minutes to rehydrate.

In a large skillet over medium-high heat, add the oil and swirl to coat the bottom of the pan. Add the onion and garlic and cook for another 5 minutes, stirring often, until the onions begin to change color. If onions are starting to stick, you can add a tablespoon or two of water or another tablespoon of oil. Add the mushrooms and cook for another 7 to 10 minutes, or until the mushrooms have softened. Add the reserved TVP and the smoked paprika, cumin, and dried garlic, stirring until well combined. Cook for another 3 minutes, stirring often so that the TVP doesn't stick, and adding an additional tablespoon of oil if needed. Add the tomato sauce, Bragg Liquid Aminos, agave nectar, and liquid smoke, stirring well until mixed. Add salt and pepper to taste. Add the cayenne to taste, stirring well. Cook for another 10 minutes, stirring as needed. Adjust seasonings to taste.

Divide the Sloppy Joe mixture equally among 4 hamburger buns and serve hot.

Tip: For a spicy kick, add a little hot sauce to the cooked Sloppy Joes mixture before serving.

Philly Seitan Sliders

Here's a fun twist on the slider–burger craze.

This version uses homemade seitan, which is fried up Philly cheesesteak–style, "wid Whiz."

MAKES 4 SLIDER
SANDWICHES

2 tablespoons olive oil, plus
more as needed

2 large bell peppers, cored,
seeded, and cut into thin
strips

2 small to medium onions,
halved and thinly sliced

Kosher salt and freshly
ground black pepper, to
taste

12 ounces thinly sliced seitan (see Pot Roast, page
000,
or Smoky Seitan Roast,
page 117)

8 dinner rolls or small hamburger buns, homemade
or store-bought, sliced in
half

Cheezy Sauce (see page
167) or vegan cheese of
your choice, as needed

Preheat the oven to 300°F.

In a large cast-iron skillet, heat the olive oil over
medium-high heat. Add the peppers and onions and
cook, stirring as needed until they are just starting to
soften, about 5 to 10 minutes. Add salt and pepper to
taste. Add the seitan and cook until lightly seared and
peppers and onions are lightly browned, about 5 to 10
minutes more.

While the peppers and onions are cooking, place the
rolls on a baking sheet and gently warm the rolls in the
oven.

Remove the warm rolls from the oven and fill with the
sautéed seitan, peppers, and onions. For a Philly-style
sandwich, drizzle with cheese sauce (or use another
cheese of your choice) and serve.

Q Sandwiches

These sandwiches are finger-licking good!

Although they make me think of summertime barbecues, they are really good anytime of the year. There's just something about that savory barbecue layered with slightly crisp coleslaw, and a nice soft bun.

MAKES ABOUT
4 SANDWICHES

1 tablespoon olive oil

1 pound Smoky Seitan (about ³/₄ of a loaf of Smoky Seitan, see page 114), thinly sliced

³/₄ cup Rough Rider Barbecue Sauce (see page 178), plus more for serving

4 hamburger buns, home-made or store-bought

1 recipe Sandwich Slaw (see page 75)

Heat a large cast-iron skillet over medium-high heat. Add the olive oil and coat the bottom of the pan. Add the seitan and cook, stirring until lightly browned. Add the barbecue sauce and cook, stirring as needed for about 5 minutes, or until the sauce is starting to caramelize and the seitan is coated. Add more barbecue sauce as needed.

Divide the hot seitan mixture among the 4 bottom halves of the hamburger buns. Drizzle with additional barbecue sauce as needed and top with a big scoop of the Sandwich Slaw. Place the top halves of the hamburger buns over the slaw and serve right away.

Mushroom Burgers

Veggie burgers come in many different incarnations, some firm and meaty, and others softer and vegetable-laden. This recipe is of the softer, vegetable-based variety, which is fantastic served up on a bun. The cashews lend a subtle sweetness and a dose of heart-healthy protein along with the tofu.

MAKES ABOUT 6 BURGERS

2 large slices of fresh bread

6 ounces (about 1 1/2 cups) sliced cremini mushrooms

2 carrots, grated (about 1 cup)

1/2 cup chopped yellow onion

1/2 cup raw cashews

7 ounces (1/2 of a 14-ounce container) firm tofu, well-drained and coarsely grated or crumbled

3 tablespoons nutritional yeast flakes

2 tablespoons Bragg Liquid Aminos or soy sauce

1/4 teaspoon fine sea salt, or to taste

Freshly ground black pepper

Brown rice flour, as needed for dusting

Olive oil, for cooking

6 hamburger buns, home-made or store-bought

Lettuce, for serving

Sliced tomato, for serving

Sliced red or sweet onion, for serving

In the bowl of a food processor, pulse the bread until finely minced. Remove the breadcrumbs to a large bowl. You should have 1 1/2 cups. Set aside.

In the food processor, finely chop the mushrooms. Transfer the mushrooms to a large, dry nonstick skillet, and cook the mushrooms over medium-high heat for several minutes to soften. Set aside.

In the food processor, combine the carrot, onion, and cashews, and pulse until finely ground. Add the cooked mushrooms and grated tofu. Pulse until just mixed. Don't purée. Transfer the mixture to the bowl of breadcrumbs. Add the nutritional yeast, liquid aminos, salt, and pepper, and stir well to combine. Adjust the seasonings to taste.

Place the brown rice flour on a small plate. Divide the burger mixture into 6 patties and dredge on all sides with rice flour.

Set a large skillet over medium-high heat and lightly coat or spray with olive oil. Cook the patties in batches if necessary on one side for 5 to 7 minutes, or until nicely browned and crispy. Add more olive oil as necessary to keep the burgers from sticking. Flip the burgers over and cook on other side until browned.

Serve the burgers on a bun with all the fixings: buns, lettuce, tomato, and onion.

Although my kids can be pretty picky when it comes to mushrooms, they don't seem to notice them in this recipe. I love that I can serve these to the whole family.

Brown Rice Hazelnut Burgers

Just one bite of these burgers makes me think of Oregon. The toasty hazelnuts, nutty rice, and earthy mushrooms are all flavors that are prevalent in dishes here. Oh, I could eat these burgers every day!

MAKES ABOUT 7 BURGERS

1 cup dried TVP or TSP granules

1 to 2 tablespoons olive oil, or as needed

8 ounces cremini mushrooms, sliced

1/2 cup diced yellow onion

3 large cloves garlic, pressed or finely minced

1 cup cooked short grain brown rice

3/4 cup coarsely chopped hazelnuts, skinned and lightly toasted

1/4 cup vital wheat gluten

1/4 cup whole wheat flour

1/4 cup freshly minced parsley

2 tablespoons chickpea flour

1 teaspoon fine sea salt, or to taste

Freshly ground black pepper, to taste

Hamburger buns, for serving

Lettuce or salad greens, for serving

Sliced tomato, for serving

Sliced onion, for serving

Preheat the oven to 350°F. Line a baking sheet with greased parchment paper or a silicone mat.

In a small saucepan, bring 3/4 cup water to a boil. Remove from the heat, stir in the TVP and cover with a lid. Set aside for 10 minutes, or until the TVP has absorbed all of the water. Set the rehydrated TVP aside to cool completely.

Heat a large skillet over medium-high heat and add the olive oil. Add the mushrooms, and sauté for 5 minutes, or until soft. Set aside to cool completely.

In the bowl of a food processor fitted with the metal blade, add the onion, garlic, and cooled mushrooms and pulse until finely chopped. Add the cooled and drained TVP mixture, along with the cooked rice and hazelnuts, and pulse again until finely chopped. Don't purée the mixture. Remove the mixture to a large mixing bowl, and add the vital wheat gluten, flour, parsley, chickpea flour, and salt and pepper, mixing until combined. You may want to use your hands, but don't overwork. Form into 7 balls, and flatten each one into 3 1/2 to 4-inch burgers. Place the burgers on the prepared baking sheet and bake for 15 minutes. Flip the burgers over and bake for another 15 minutes on the other side.

Serve the burgers on a bun with all the fixings: lettuce, tomato, and onion.

You'll want to prep ahead for this recipe. Of course it's easiest if you have leftover brown rice in your fridge from dinner the night before, but if you don't, plan on the rice taking about 50 minutes to cook. While the rice cooks, you can toast the hazelnuts and sauté the mushrooms.

Quinoa Burgers

This burger is loaded with nutritious ingredients,
making it a powerhouse burger that's delicious, too. The poultry seasoning contributes
great flavor, with its savory blend of rosemary, sage, marjoram, nutmeg, and black pepper.

MAKES ABOUT
6 BURGERS

1/2 cup diced yellow onion

3 cloves garlic

12 ounces chickpeas (about
  1 1/2 cups), canned or
  homemade, drained

1/2 cup quick oats
  (not instant)

1 1/2 cups cooked quinoa

1/4 cup minced fresh parsley

1 teaspoon poultry seasoning or favorite spice blend

1 teaspoon smoked paprika

2 tablespoons Bragg Liquid
  Aminos or soy sauce

2 tablespoons chickpea
  flour

1/2 teaspoon salt, or to taste

Freshly ground black
  pepper, to taste

Brown rice flour or whole
  wheat or all-purpose
  flour, for dusting

Olive oil, for cooking

Hamburger buns, for
  serving

Lettuce or salad greens,
  for serving

Sliced tomato, for serving

Sliced onion, for serving

In bowl of a food processor, add the onion and garlic and pulse until finely chopped. Add the chickpeas and oats, and pulse until well mixed. Don't purée the mixture. Remove the mixture to a large mixing bowl, and stir in the quinoa, parsley, poultry seasoning, smoked paprika, Bragg Liquid Aminos, and chickpea flour. Stir in 1 to 2 tablespoons water, if needed to help the burger mixture stick together, although you don't want to make the mixture too moist. Add salt and pepper to taste. Thoroughly mix the ingredients well, cover the bowl and refrigerate for 15 minutes. Form the burger mixture into 6 balls, and press into 3 1/2 to 4-inch patties.

Heat a large cast-iron skillet over medium-high heat, and lightly coat or spray with olive oil. Place the brown rice flour on a small plate and dust the burgers on all sides with the rice flour. Add the burgers to the hot skillet. Cook the patties for about 5 minutes, or until nicely browned and crispy. Reduce the heat to medium, if necessary, to continue cooking without burning. Add more olive oil as necessary, to keep the burgers from sticking. Flip the burgers over and cook on other side. Repeat with the remaining burgers.

Remove the burgers from the skillet and let sit for 5 minutes before serving. Letting the burgers rest will give them a better texture.

Serve the burgers on a bun with all the fixings: lettuce, tomato, and onion.

To cook quinoa, combine 1 cup of dry, rinsed quinoa with 2 cups of water. Bring to a boil in a large saucepan, reduce heat to low, cover, and simmer for 15 minutes.

Grilled Cheezy Sandwiches

I have an ongoing love affair with this sandwich.

It is total comfort food with the warm, creamy, melty center and the crisp and buttery crust. Try it served alongside a bowl of tomato soup for lunch!

MAKES 4 SANDWICHES

8 slices rustic, French, or sourdough bread

Homemade Great Smoky Mountain Cheeze (see page 168)

1 large beefsteak tomato, sliced

1 small sweet onion, thinly sliced

Non-hydrogenated vegan margarine, softened, as needed

On four of the slices of bread, spread 2 to 4 table-spoons (depending on your preference and the size of the slice) of the Homemade Great Smoky Mountain Cheeze. Top with a single layer of tomato and onion slices. Top with remaining slices of bread and close sandwiches. Coat both sides of sandwiches with a light spread of margarine.

Heat a large nonstick skillet over medium heat. Add sandwiches to the skillet, in batches if necessary. Cook for about 3 minutes on each side, or until the bread is lightly toasted and cheese is warm. Repeat with remaining sandwiches. Serve the sandwiches warm.

Variation: If you don't have time to make the homemade cheese, you can substitute store-bought non-dairy cheese. I really like the Daiya brand in this recipe.

You can have immense fun customizing this grilled cheese sandwich. Here are a couple of ideas: omit the sliced onions and sprinkle on some Fakin' Bakin' Bits (see page 175) and thinly sliced scallions along with the tomato. You can also layer on some Smoky Curls (see page 76) or use store-bought vegan white cheese and a big smear of Basil and Spinach Spread (see page 174).

Cheezy Mac

Here is my kid-approved, cheese-less version of creamy mac-and-cheese. Feel free to customize this dish even further by sprinkling the top with smoked paprika or spice it up with some finely diced jalapeños. This is a variation of the mac-and-cheese special served at our food cart, Native Bowl, which has proven so popular that we had to add it to our regular menu.

MAKES ABOUT 4 SERVINGS

10 ounces dried macaroni

$1/2$ cup raw cashews

6 tablespoons nutritional yeast flakes, divided

2 tablespoons cornstarch

2 tablespoons unbleached all-purpose flour

2 teaspoons granulated garlic

$1^1/2$ teaspoons granulated onion

$1^1/4$ teaspoons smoked paprika

$1^1/4$ teaspoons fine sea salt

$1/2$ teaspoon sweet or regular paprika

1 tablespoon non-hydro-genated vegan margarine

In a large pot of lightly salted boiling water, add the pasta shells and cook according to package directions until al dente, about 10 minutes. Drain the pasta well, return to the pot, and cover with lid to keep warm.

In the jar of a blender, combine $2^1/2$ cups water and cashews. Blend the mixture at high speed until completely smooth and no bits of nuts remain. Add 5 tablespoons of nutritional yeast, cornstarch, flour, garlic, onion, smoked paprika, salt, and paprika, blending until very smooth.

Transfer the mixture to a large saucepan and place over medium heat. Bring sauce to a simmer, whisking continuously. Once mixture comes to a simmer, reduce heat slightly and cook, whisking continuously until thickened, about 3 to 5 minutes.

Pour the cheesy sauce over the cooked pasta shells, mixing until the pasta is coated. Add the margarine and remaining 1 tablespoon nutritional yeast flakes, stirring until mixed. Add salt and pepper to taste. Serve hot.

Variation: For a gluten-free recipe, replace the shells with an equal amount of corn, brown rice, or quinoa pasta.

Tip: If you don't have a powerful blender, soak the cashews in hot water to cover for 30 minutes. Drain and proceed with the directions above.

For a truly cheesy texture, stir about a $1/2$ cup or so of non-dairy cheese into the hot pasta mixture.. My favorite brand of non-dairy cheese is Daiya.

Jambalaya

When you want a quick weeknight meal that will make your taste buds sing, this is your dish. I love serving a big ol' pot of this for company, as all of the work can be done before your guests arrive, simmering away while you enjoy your guests. Although you might be tempted to substitute brown rice, this dish comes out best with long grain white rice.

MAKES 6 TO 8 SERVINGS

- 1 tablespoon extra-virgin olive oil
- 1 large onion, sliced into $1/4$-inch crescents
- 4 cloves garlic, smashed, pressed or minced
- 2 green bell peppers, chopped
- 4 ribs celery, cut into $1/4$-inch slices
- 2 vegetarian sausages, sliced into rounds
- $1^1/4$ cups of long grain white rice, not rinsed
- 1 (29-ounce) can diced tomatoes, drained, preferably organic
- 2 cups vegetable broth or hot water with 1 vegetarian bouillon cube or 1 tablespoon broth powder
- 1 tablespoon Creole seasoning (with salt added), or more to taste (*see note*)
- $1^1/2$ teaspoon smoked paprika
- Salt and pepper, optional, to taste

Heat the oil in a large Dutch oven or heavy pot with a lid over medium-high heat. Add the onion, garlic, peppers, celery, and sausage and sauté until lightly browned and slightly softened. Add the rice and sauté for 1 minute more. Add the tomatoes, broth, Creole seasoning (see tip below), and paprika, stirring well.

Bring the mixture to a boil, reduce the heat, cover, and simmer for about 30 minutes, or until the rice is tender and most of the liquid has been absorbed. Add salt and pepper to taste.

Remove the pot from heat and let sit, covered, for 10 minutes. Serve the jambalaya hot.

For the Creole seasoning: I really like Tony Chachere's Original Creole Seasoning in this recipe. I usually add 2 to 3 tablespoons (rather than 1), but it gives it a big kick, so you have to add it to taste.

Black-Eyed Peas

Here's is a real down-home dish: a hearty bean stew of sorts.
Serve the peas atop freshly cooked brown or white rice, and you've got a great, filling dinner.
I like to take it a step further and sprinkle mine generously with hot sauce.

MAKES ABOUT
4 TO 6 SERVINGS

2 cups dried black-eyed peas, rinsed well and picked over

1/2 small onion, finely chopped

1 large green bell pepper, finely chopped

3 stalks celery, sliced into 1/4-inch pieces

4 garlic cloves, minced or pressed

1 bay leaf

1 tablespoon vegetarian chicken bouillon powder, or 1 large vegetable bouillon cube

2 1/2 teaspoons Creole or Cajun seasoning (with salt), or to taste *(see note on page 105)*

Freshly ground black pepper, to taste

Cooked brown or white rice, for serving

In a large pot, combine 8 cups of water, the black-eyed peas, onion, green bell pepper, celery, garlic, and the bay leaf. Bring to a boil over medium-high heat. Once the mixture comes to a boil, reduce the heat, cover the pot partially with a lid, and simmer for 30 to 40 minutes, or until the peas are tender.

Stir in the bouillon powder, Cajun seasoning, and pepper to taste. Serve the hot black-eyed peas over cooked brown or white rice.

Variation: Once the peas are tender, stir in half of a 15-ounce can (or more to taste) of diced tomatoes, and cook for 10 additional minutes.

The Blue Plate Special

This savory waffles and gravy recipe really came about by accident. It was late in the afternoon, and I hadn't yet decided what to make for dinner. Since I was testing savory breakfast recipes, I thought it might be fun to serve them for dinner as a blue plate special. My family devoured the entire meal before I could even sit down at the table.

MAKES 2 TO 4 SERVINGS

Savory Cornbread Waffles (see variation, page 37)

Smoky Potato Scramble (see page 44)

Double recipe of Creamy Sage and Pepper Gravy (see page 160)

Ground paprika, for garnish

Place 1 or 2 warm waffles on each plate, depending on how hearty you want your servings to be. Top each waffle with a quarter of the scramble. Generously ladle hot gravy over the potato scramble, and sprinkle with a touch of paprika.

Serve the waffles and gravy hot.

Tip: If desired, the waffles can be made ahead of time. Simply reheat by popping them in the toaster oven for a couple of minutes to warm and recrisp.

Veggies and Dumplings

An old-fashioned favorite that tastes just like Grandma's

will cure what ails you. There's nothing quite like a warm bowl of this in
the winter to keep you warm. It can easily be made in less than 40 minutes.

MAKES 4 TO 6 SERVINGS

Stew

3 tablespoons vegetarian chicken or vegetable bouillon powder (or less if you have a saltier brand)

3 tablespoons nutritional yeast flakes

2 teaspoons granulated onion or onion powder

4 large carrots cut into rounds

4 ribs celery, cut into slices

1 small yellow or white onion, finely diced

2 cups fresh or frozen chopped broccoli

1/2 cup unbleached all-purpose flour

1/2 cup plain, unsweetened soymilk

1 tablespoon dried parsley flakes or 2 to 3 tablespoons minced fresh parsley

1 teaspoon fine sea salt, or to taste

Freshly ground black pepper to taste

1 cup frozen peas

For the stew: In a large pot or Dutch oven, combine 6 cups water, bouillon powder, nutritional yeast flakes, granulated onion, carrots, celery, and onion. Bring to a simmer over medium-high heat. Reduce heat to maintain a slow simmer, partially cover, and cook for 20 minutes, or until vegetables are just tender. If using fresh broccoli, stir it in now.

Using a blender or immersion blender, combine the flour, soymilk, and 1/2 cup water. Blend until smooth. Slowly whisk the flour mixture into the vegetable stew. Continue whisking until the soup is thickened. Whisk in the dried parsley. Add salt and pepper to taste. Whisking continuously, bring to a simmer. If using frozen broccoli, stir it into the pot now with the peas.

For the dumplings: In a medium bowl, combine flour, baking powder, and salt, mixing well. Add the soymilk and oil, stirring until dough is moistened and just comes together. Do not overmix.

Drop the dumpling dough by small spoonfuls one at a time into the thickened stew. Do not stir. Cover the pot, reduce the heat, and simmer for 15 minutes. Make sure not to peek or remove the lid, as the dumplings need to steam. After 15 minutes, uncover pot and check to make sure the dumplings are cooked through by removing one dumpling and cutting through the middle. If not, cover pot and simmer for another 5 minutes. Sprinkle dill over top, if using, and ladle the stew and dumplings into bowls. Serve right away.

Dumplings

- **2 cups all-purpose flour**
- **1 tablespoon baking powder**
- **$^1/_2$ teaspoon fine sea salt**
- **$^3/_4$ cup plus 2 tablespoons plain unsweetened soymilk or non-dairy milk of choice**
- **2 tablespoons canola oil**
- **Dried or fresh minced dill for garnish (optional)**

Variation: For an extra-hearty soup, add 1 to 1$^1/_2$ cups diced seitan or 2 ounces (1 cup) dried Soy Curls: reconstitute the Soy Curls in 1 cup hot water and 2 teaspoons vegetarian chicken bouillon powder (or to taste).

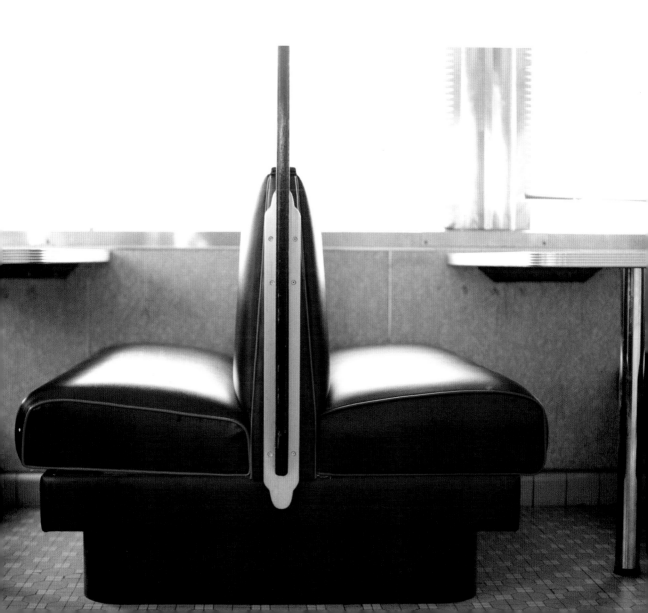

Skillet–Baked Panko Cutlets

Cutlets are the ultimate in comfort food, and a dish that I often serve to company. We love it topped with vegan mozzarella, thought's just as scrumptious without. I've adapted this recipe from one that I created for the Everyday Dish website.

MAKES 6 SERVINGS

Sauce

1 (28-ounce) can tomato sauce

1 (28-ounce) can diced tomatoes

1 tablespoon fresh oregano, minced or 1 teaspoon dried oregano

4 cloves garlic, pressed or finely minced

$^1/_3$ cup minced fresh parsley, plus more for garnish

Breading

$^3/_4$ cup whole wheat or all-purpose flour

1 tablespoon nutritional yeast flakes

$^1/_2$ teaspoon granulated garlic

Pinch sea salt

Freshly ground pepper

$^2/_3$ cup plain soymilk

4 tablespoons cornstarch

$1^1/_2$ cups unseasoned panko breadcrumbs, plus more as needed

9 Italian Sausage Cutlets (see page 119)

2 to 4 tablespoons olive oil, for cooking

$^1/_2$ to 1 cup shredded vegan mozzarella (optional)

For the sauce: In a large saucepan, combine the tomato sauce, diced tomatoes, oregano, and garlic. With a stick or immersion blender, blend all of the ingredients together. Alternately, you can blend everything in a blender or food processor and then pour into the saucepan. Stir in $^1/_3$ cup minced parsley. Bring to a simmer and cook over medium heat while you prepare the cutlets.

For the cutlets: On a large plate or pie dish, mix together the flour, nutritional yeast flakes, garlic, salt, and pepper. Set aside.

In a shallow bowl, whisk together the soymilk and cornstarch until smooth.

On a large plate or pie dish, add the panko breadcrumbs. Working with one cutlet at a time, lightly coat each side of cutlet with seasoned flour. Next, dip the cutlets into the soymilk mixture, coating cutlets on both sides. Finally, coat the cutlets with the panko breadcrumbs, making sure to coat both sides well. Repeat with remaining cutlets.

Place a large cast-iron or ovenproof skillet over medium-high heat. Add a tablespoon or two of oil to the skillet, tilting the pan to spread the oil in an even layer. Add cutlets and cook for 3 to 4 minutes, until lightly browned and crisp on the bottom. Flip cutlets over, cooking another 3 to 4 minutes until lightly browned and crisp on the other side. Reduce heat slightly if the cutlets start to burn. Remove the breaded cutlets to a plate and repeat with the remaining cutlets, adding additional oil as necessary.

Return half of the cutlets to the skillet. Pour half of the hot tomato sauce on top of the cutlets. Top with the rest of the cutlets, followed by the remaining sauce. Sprinkle the shredded cheese on top of tomato sauce. Place the skillet under the broiler until the cheese is golden (and melted if using mozzarella) for several minutes. Watch carefully so that cheese doesn't burn. Alternatively, you can serve the tomato sauce on the side as one of my testers did (thanks, Kim!). Return all of the cutlets to the skillet and top with shredded cheese. Broil as directed. Serve the sauce on the side at the table.

Remove skillet from oven, sprinkle with additional minced parsley and serve.

Tip: This recipe can easily be cut in half. For the sauce, substitute 15–ounce cans of diced tomatoes and tomato sauce but leave all other ingredients as is.

Barbecued Ribz

I bet that you thought vegan ribs were impossible.
Well think again! You'll be amazed at just how awesome they are.
Believe it or not, the ribs are even better the next day. This recipe was
created by Susan Voisin of the Fat Free Vegan Kitchen blog.

MAKES 2 TO 4 SERVINGS

1 cup vital wheat gluten

2 teaspoons smoked paprika

2 tablespoons nutritional yeast

2 teaspoons onion powder

1 teaspoon garlic powder

1 teaspoon fine sea salt

2 tablespoons creamy peanut butter, tahini, or other nut butter

1 teaspoon liquid smoke

Preheat the oven to 350°F. Lightly spray an 8 x 8-inch baking dish with canola oil.

In a large bowl, combine the vital wheat gluten, smoked paprika, nutritional yeast flakes, onion powder, garlic powder, and fine sea salt, mixing well.

In a bowl or measuring cup, mix together $3/4$ cup cool water with the peanut butter until smooth. Add the liquid smoke and soy sauce, mixing well. Add the peanut butter mixture to the dry ingredients. Stir to mix well and then knead lightly in the bowl for a minute or two.

Put the dough into the baking dish and flatten it so that it evenly fills the pan. Take a sharp knife and cut it into 8 strips; then turn the pan 90 degrees and cut

1 tablespoon soy sauce

1 cup of Rough Rider Barbecue Sauce (see page 178) or favorite store-bought sauce, plus more as needed

those strips in half to form 16 pieces.

Bake the ribz for 30 minutes. (They should only be partially cooked at this point.) While they're cooking, prepare your outdoor grill or grill pan.

Remove the ribz from the oven and carefully score each strip, partially cutting them to make sure that they'll pull apart easily later. You don't want to separate each rib, just score them so that they will come apart easily when serving. Generously brush the top with barbecue sauce.

Take the ribz to the grill or grill pan and invert the whole dish onto the grill (or use a large spatula to lift the ribz out, placing it sauce-side down on the grill). Brush the top with more sauce.

Watch the ribz closely to make sure that they don't burn. When sufficiently brown and caramelized on one side, turn over and cook the other side, adding more sauce, if necessary. When done, remove to a platter and cut or pull apart the individual ribz to serve.

Tip: These ribz are even better the next day, after resting in the refrigerator overnight. Try serving them warm, as is, with a big salad, cooked greens, or potato salad. They also make an awesome sandwich topped with coleslaw.

Smoky Seitan Roast

This smoky flavored seitan roast is what I use
in the Q sandwiches. It's great smothered in barbeque sauce, but
also delicious thinly sliced and served on sandwiches.

MAKES 1 LARGE LOAF

2 cups vital wheat gluten

1/2 cup nutritional yeast flakes

1/4 cup chickpea flour

1 tablespoon granulated onion or onion powder

1 tablespoon porcini mushroom powder, optional

2 teaspoons granulated garlic or garlic powder

2 teaspoons smoked paprika

1 teaspoon fine sea salt

1/2 teaspoon ground white pepper

1/2 teaspoon coarsely ground black pepper

2 cups cool water, plus more as needed

2 tablespoons soy sauce

1 tablespoon toasted sesame oil

1 tablespoon liquid smoke

In a large bowl, mix together the vital wheat gluten, nutritional yeast flakes, chickpea flour, granulated onion, porcini mushroom powder, granulated garlic, smoked paprika, salt, and white and black peppers. In a large measuring cup or pitcher, whisk together the cool water, soy sauce, sesame oil, and liquid smoke, and gently stir into the dry ingredients. The dough should be moist. If it's dry, add another tablespoon of water as needed. Stir just until ingredients are mixed.

Shape the dough into a roast shape, about the size of a loaf pan, and wrap in a damp tea towel. Tie up the ends with white cotton string. Fill the bottom of a steamer with water and heat until simmering. Place the roast in the top of the steamer, cover and steam for 45 to 50 minutes or until firm. If a steamer is unavailable to you, you can place a small collapsible steamer insert in a large stock pot, with simmering water underneath. Uncover the pot and let stand 5 minutes. Alternatively, you can wrap the roast in a large piece of aluminum foil, twisting the ends well to seal. Although you want to wrap it well, don't cover in too many layers of foil or else the steam won't penetrate the roast. If steaming the roast in foil, steam for 60 minutes, open foil and steam again for an additional 5 minutes or until fairly firm to the touch.

Carefully remove roast from the steamer to a cutting board. Unwrap the roast from the tea towel or foil. Let roast cool on the board and refrigerate until ready to use. Let roast cool on the board and refrigerate in a covered container (or zip-top bag) until ready to use.

Tip: The seitan will firm up further after being refrigerated overnight. If you let the roast cool too long before unwrapping, the towel will stick, causing the roast to tear. If you find this happening, simply moisten the towel with water, which should help prevent the tearing.

Pastrami–Style Seitan Roast

Who says you can't have vegan pastrami? This recipe proves you can! The brilliant idea of flavoring the roast with caraway and fennel is thanks to the creative mind of cookbook author and friend Brian P. McCarthy, whose Seitan Corned Beef inspired this recipe.

MAKES 1 LARGE ROAST

2 cups vital wheat gluten

1/2 cup nutritional yeast flakes

1/2 cup chickpea flour

2 tablespoons granulated onion or onion powder

1 tablespoon paprika

2 teaspoons granulated garlic or garlic powder

1 tablespoon fennel seeds, finely ground

1 tablespoon caraway seeds, finely ground

2 teaspoons fine sea salt

2 cups cool tap water

3 tablespoons olive oil

2 tablespoons red wine vinegar

About 1 tablespoon coarsely ground pepper, or as needed

In a large bowl, mix together the vital wheat gluten, nutritional yeast flakes, chickpea flour, granulated onion, paprika, granulated garlic, ground fennel, ground caraway, and salt. In a large measuring cup or pitcher, whisk together the water, olive oil, and red wine vinegar, and gently stir into the dry ingredients. The dough should be moist. If it's dry, add another tablespoon or two of water as needed. Stir just until ingredients are mixed.

Shape the dough into a roast shape, sprinkle with coarsely ground pepper, coating lightly, and wrap in a damp tea towel. Tie up the ends with white cotton string. Fill the bottom of a steamer with water and heat until simmering. Place the roast in the top of the steamer and steam for 45 to 50 minutes or until firm. If a steamer is unavailable to you, you can place a small collapsible steamer insert in a large stock pot, with simmering water underneath. Place the roast in the steamer, cover and steam for 50 minutes or until firm to the touch. Uncover the pot and let stand for 5 minutes. Alternatively, you can wrap the roast in a large piece of aluminum foil, being careful not to roll too tight as it

(continued on next page)

needs a little room to expand. Twist the ends well to seal. Although you want to wrap it well, don't cover in too many layers of foil or else the steam won't penetrate the roast. If steaming the roast in foil, steam for 60 minutes, open foil and steam again for an additional 5 minutes or until fairly firm to the touch.

Carefully remove the roast from the steamer to a cutting board. Unwrap the roast from the tea towel or foil. Let the roast cool on the board and refrigerate until ready to use. Slice the roast very thinly for sandwiches.

Tip: The seitan will firm up further after being refrigerated overnight. If you let the roast cool too long before unwrapping it, the cloth will stick, causing the roast to tear. If you find this happening, simply moisten the towel with water, which should help prevent the tearing.
I make this seitan so much now that I invested in a home meat slicer. It gives you super-thin slices that resemble professional deli-sliced meats. The electric slicers are not expensive, especially if you look at stores like Costco, or search online. We use it all the time, although we now refer to it as our "seitan slicer."

Tip: I like using the vital wheat gluten from Bob's Red Mill in all of my seitan recipes.

Not Your Mama's Pot Roast with Roasted Vegetables

Many of us have slow cookers in our cabinets, but they often get little use. At least this is true in my house. Figuring that a slow cooker would probably be great for seitan, I got to work. This is a homey seitan roast, with lots of delicious vegetables cooked alongside.

MAKES 1 ROAST,
OR 4 TO 6 SERVINGS

Vegetables

1½ cups vegetable stock or 1 tablespoon vegetarian chicken or vegetable bouillon powder plus 1½ cups water

2 tablespoons soy sauce (reduce to 1 tablespoon if using a salty broth)

3 to 4 garlic cloves, crushed

1 sprig fresh thyme or ¼ teaspoon dried whole thyme

1 sprig fresh rosemary or ¼ teaspoon dried ground rosemary

Salt and freshly ground black pepper

1½ pounds small red-skinned potatoes, cut into chunks

1 small yellow onion, peeled and sliced

2 cups chopped carrots (about 1-inch pieces)

Roast

2 cups vital wheat gluten

¼ cup nutritional yeast flakes

(continued)

For the vegetables: Mix together the vegetable stock, soy sauce, garlic, thyme, rosemary, and salt and pepper to taste. Toss with the the potatoes, onions, and carrots in a mixing bowl and set aside.

For the roast: in a large bowl, combine the wheat gluten, nutritional yeast, chickpea flour, mushroom powder, granulated onion, granulated garlic, salt, and pepper, whisking well. In a large measuring cup or bowl, whisk together the water, olive oil, soy sauce, Marmite, and garlic. Add the water mixture to the dry ingredients, adding a little more water as needed if the mixture is too dry. Using your hands, mix the dough in the bowl until well mixed and smooth. You will start to see the strands of gluten starting to form. Shape the gluten into a loaf and place in the bottom of a lightly oiled slow cooker. Pour the vegetables and stock on top. Put the lid on the slow cooker and cook on high for 4 hours, or until the seitan is firm to the touch and the vegetables are cooked. The seitan will spread some across the bottom of the slow-cooker.

To serve, remove the vegetables and seitan from the slow cooker. Cut the seitan into slices and arrange them on a serving platter. Surround with the vegetables and spoon the cooking liquid over all.

(continued on next page)

- $^1/_4$ cup chickpea flour
- 1 tablespoon porcini mushroom powder (*see note*)
- 1 tablespoon granulated onion
- 1 tablespoon granulated garlic
- 1 teaspoon fine sea salt
- $^1/_2$ teaspoon coarsely ground pepper
- $1^3/_4$ cups cool tap water
- 2 tablespoons olive oil
- 3 tablespoons soy sauce
- 2 tablespoons Marmite yeast paste (*see note*)
- 4 cloves garlic, pressed or finely minced

Porcini mushroom powder is a wonderful ingredient, which can add additional flavor to recipes. It can be found online, but you can also make it at home with a strong blender and dried porcini slices. Wipe any dirt or debris off the dried mushroom pieces and add to a blender jar. Whiz them for several minutes until they are pulverized and powdered. Marmite can be found at well-stocked grocery and specialty stores (and online). Marmite is a yeast extract and also a nutritious savory spread, full of B vitamins. I like to use it to give a nice savory beefy-flavor to seitan and broths. If you can't find Marmite, you could try substituting red miso in the recipe.

Italian Sausage Cutlets

This recipe is adapted from my sausage recipe
on the Everyday Dish website. These cutlets are meant to be used in the
recipe for Skillet–Baked Panko Cutlets (see page110). The cutlets freeze really
well, so you may want to make a double batch and freeze the extras.

MAKES 9 TO 10 CUTLETS

2 cups vital wheat gluten

¼ cup nutritional yeast
flakes

¼ cup chickpea flour

2 tablespoons granulated
onion or onion powder

1 tablespoon fennel seed
(optional)

2 teaspoons granulated garlic or garlic powder

1 teaspoon coarsely ground
pepper, preferably freshly
ground

1 teaspoon dried chili flakes,
optional

1 teaspoon ground smoked
paprika

1 teaspoon dried oregano

2 teaspoons salt

2 cups cool water

3 tablespoons olive oil

2 tablespoons soy sauce

Fill the bottom of a large steamer with water and pre-heat. Alternatively, fill the bottom of a large pot with a little water and use a collapsible steamer insert.

In a large bowl, combine the vital wheat gluten, nutritional yeast flakes, chickpea flour, granulated onion, fennel, granulated garlic, black pepper, chili flakes, smoked paprika, dried oregano, and salt, mixing well.

In a large measuring cup or medium bowl, use a fork to whisk together the water, olive oil, and soy sauce and gently stir into the dry ingredients. Stir just until ingredients are mixed. If dough mixture is too dry, you can add another tablespoon of water or as needed.

Scoop ⅓ cup dough mixture at a time and shape into thin patties, about 4 to 4½ inches across. Place the patties on a piece of aluminum foil (there's no need to wrap them up). Fill the bottom of a steamer with water and heat until simmering. Place the cutlets in steamer. It's okay to stack them so that they are over-lapping a little, but try to keep them as flat as possible since they will remain in whatever shape that they steam in. Cover the steamer and steam the sausages for 45 minutes, or until they are firm to the touch. Remove the steamer from the heat and remove the lid of the steamer so that the cutlets can cool for 10 minutes.

Once the cutlets have cooled down slightly, remove them from the foil and transfer to a plate to cool completely. Once they are cool, refrigerate the cutlets until ready to eat. After cooling, they may feel a bit dry on the outside. Don't worry, as they will firm up considerably after chilling.

Home-Style Loaf

This savory loaf reminds me a lot of my mom's meatloaf,
especially served alongside fluffy mashed potatoes and lots of gravy. If you are lucky
enough to have any leftovers the following day, it makes an awesome
sandwich with some good rustic whole grain bread.

MAKES 1 LOAF

10 ounces firm tofu

$1/2$ yellow onion, finely chopped

1 cup finely chopped celery

3 cloves garlic, pressed

1 (12-ounce) package vegan soy crumbles, refrigerated or frozen

$1^1/_4$ cups quick oats

1 cup raw walnut halves, finely ground in food processor

3 tablespoons soy sauce

$1/2$ cup ketchup, divided

2 tablespoons stone-ground mustard

2 teaspoons dry sage or poultry seasoning

$1/2$ cup minced fresh parsley

Salt and freshly ground pepper, to taste

Preheat oven to 350°F. Lightly grease a 9 x 5-inch loaf pan with olive, vegetable, or canola oil.

Rinse the tofu and pat dry with a paper towel to absorb any extra water. Crumble the tofu into a large bowl, or grate using the holes of a large grater. Add the chopped onion, celery, garlic, soy crumbles, oats, walnuts, soy sauce, $1/4$ cup ketchup, mustard, sage, and parsley. Stir until well mixed. Add salt and ground pepper to taste.

Scoop the mixture into the prepared loaf pan, lightly packing it in and smoothing the top. Spread the remaining $1/4$ cup of ketchup into a thin layer over top of the loaf, and place in the oven.

Bake the loaf for 55 to 60 minutes, or until the loaf is firm. Remove loaf from the oven and let cool for at least 20 minutes before serving. If serving the loaf the next day, let cool completely, cover, and refrigerate until ready to eat.

Tip: Although you may be tempted to sauté the veggies before adding them to the mixture, it's not necessary. The veggies will soften and cook while the loaf is baking.

Chicken-Style Seitan Roast

This roast is both fantastic and versatile. You can thinly slice it and serve on sandwiches, sauté in a hot skillet or even batter and fry it. This is a recipe that you'll find yourself reaching for over and over again. See the tip on page 116 for help wrapping and slicing the roast.

MAKES 1 LARGE ROAST

2 cups vital wheat gluten

$1/2$ cup nutritional yeast flakes

$1/4$ cup chickpea flour

1 tablespoon poultry seasoning

1 tablespoon granulated onion or onion powder

1 teaspoon fine sea salt

$1/2$ teaspoon ground white pepper

2 cups cool water

1 tablespoon olive oil

1 tablespoon soy sauce

In a large bowl, mix together the vital wheat gluten, nutritional yeast flakes, chickpea flour, poultry seasoning, granulated onion, salt, and white pepper.

In a large measuring cup or pitcher, whisk together the water, olive oil, and soy sauce, and gently stir into the dry ingredients. Stir just until ingredients are mixed.

Shape the dough into a roast shape and wrap in a damp tea towel or a double layer of dampened cheesecloth, tying the ends with cotton twine. Fill the bottom of a steamer with water and heat until simmering. Place the roast in the steamer, cover, and steam for 45 to 50 minutes or until firm to the touch. If a steamer is unavailable to you, you can place a small collapsible steamer insert in a large stock pot, with simmering water underneath. Alternatively, you can wrap the roast in a large piece of aluminum foil, twisting the ends to seal. Although you want to wrap it well, don't cover in too many layers of foil or else the steam won't be able to penetrate the roast. If steaming the roast in foil, steam for 60 minutes, open foil and steam again for an additional 5 minutes. The roast should be fairly firm to the touch. Uncover the steamer and let stand 5 minutes.

Carefully remove the roast from the steamer to a cutting board. Unwrap. Let the roast cool on the board and refrigerate in a covered container until ready to use.

Desserts

Soft and Chewy Chocolate Chip Cookies

I dare you to eat just one! These cookies have quickly become our family's favorite, which says a lot. We're a very tough crowd to please when it comes to chocolate chip cookies. These babies are soft and chewy, and take only minutes to whip together. They also happen to be much lower in fat than traditional chocolate chip cookies.

MAKES ABOUT
18 COOKIES

1 cup unbleached all-purpose flour

1 teaspoon baking powder

$1/2$ teaspoon baking soda

Dash of fine sea salt

$3/4$ cup lightly packed light brown sugar

3 tablespoons canola oil

2 tablespoons soymilk or other non-dairy milk

1 tablespoon flaxseed meal, preferably golden

1 tablespoon pure vanilla extract

$3/4$ cup nondairy semisweet chocolate chips

Preheat the oven to 350°F. Line 2 baking sheets with parchment paper or Silpat silicone baking mats.

In a small bowl, whisk together the flour, baking powder, baking soda, and salt. In a large bowl, beat together the brown sugar, oil, soymilk, flaxseed meal, and vanilla until smooth. Add the flour mixture to the sugar mixture, stirring just until mixed. Fold in the chocolate chips.

Using a small cookie scoop or tablespoon, scoop the batter onto the prepared baking sheets, 2 inches apart. Bake in the preheated oven for 12 minutes, or until puffed and golden brown. Remove the trays from the oven and place on a rack to cool completely.

Variation: Chocolate chip cookies are always open to a little customization. Do you love walnuts or pecans in your cookies? Throw a handful of toasted nuts into the batter. Are you crazy for citrus? Add a little freshly grated orange zest into the batter for a real taste sensation. Like raisins with your chocolate? Add a handful of dark raisins along with the chocolate chips. Who knew that cookies could be so much fun?

Oatmeal Raisin Cookies

This oatmeal cookie recipe is one of my favorites.
It's perfect with a big glass of ice-cold almond milk.
I baked up a batch as a gift for my mailman, and now every time I see
him he asks for more. Now that's the sign of a good cookie!

MAKES ABOUT 16 COOKIES

- 1$\frac{3}{4}$ cups whole wheat pastry flour
- 1$\frac{1}{2}$ teaspoons baking powder
- $\frac{3}{4}$ teaspoon baking soda
- $\frac{1}{8}$ teaspoon fine sea salt
- 1 cup plus 2 tablespoons packed light brown sugar
- 1 stick ($\frac{1}{2}$ cup) non-hydrogenated vegan margarine, softened
- 1 tablespoon pure vanilla extract
- 3 tablespoons soymilk or almond milk
- 1 tablespoon flaxseed meal, preferably golden
- 1$\frac{1}{2}$ cups old-fashioned rolled oats
- 1 cup raisins or dried cherries

Preheat the oven to 350°F. Line 2 baking sheets with parchment paper or a Silpat silicone mat.

In a small bowl, combine the flour, baking powder, baking soda, and salt,

In a large bowl of a stand mixer, beat together the brown sugar, margarine, and vanilla until light and fluffy. Add the soymilk and flax, beating until smooth. Add the flour mixture to the margarine mixture, beating just until mixed. Add the oats, mixing until incorporated. Mix in the raisins. Don't overbeat the batter.

Scoop the dough with a cookie scoop or $\frac{1}{4}$ cup measuring cup onto prepared baking sheets. Press the tops of the cookies lightly with slightly damp fingers, to flatten into a disc. Bake in the preheated oven for 14 to 15 minutes, or until the cookies have puffed up and are golden, but are still soft to the touch. They will probably have a few cracks on the top, too. Let the cookies cool completely on baking sheet before removing.

As a perfectionist cookie baker, I have a few tips and tricks to keep cookies coming out perfectly every time. The first is to not overbeat your batter, once the flour mixture is added. This will help keep your cookies from flattening out on the cookie sheet. Another pro tip is the cookie scoop, otherwise known as a dasher. Your cookies will bake and be shaped more evenly. You can find them in cooking stores, in restaurant supply stores, and online. Finally, line your cookie sheets with parchment paper or silicone mats. No greasing required, and they won't get too brown on the bottoms (unless you overbake them).

Ooey-Gooey Brownies

I spent many months on this recipe, trying to create
the perfect brownie. It had to be moist and chewy, a little fudgy but not cakey,
and most of all it had to scream "Chocolate!" As you can see, I take my brownies
very seriously. Now, what are you waiting for? Go bake some brownies!

MAKES ONE
8-INCH SQUARE PAN

Brownies

1 cup unbleached all-
   purpose flour

1/2 cup Dutch process cocoa
   powder, sifted

1 tablespoon finely ground
   coffee

1 teaspoon baking powder

1/8 teaspoon fine sea salt

3/4 cup packed light
   brown sugar

2 tablespoons granulated
   sugar

1 tablespoon cornstarch

1/3 cup vanilla soymilk

1/4 cup plain soy yogurt

1/3 cup canola oil

1 tablespoon pure
   vanilla extract

1/4 teaspoon pure
   almond extract

1/2 cup nondairy semisweet
   chocolate chips

Glaze

3/4 cup nondairy semisweet
   chocolate chips

1/4 cup vanilla soymilk

Preheat oven to 350°F. Grease an 8 x 8-inch square glass pan well with shortening.

For the brownies: In a small bowl, whisk together the flour, cocoa powder, ground coffee, baking powder, and salt. In a large bowl, whisk together the brown sugar, granulated sugar, cornstarch, soymilk, soy yogurt, oil, vanilla, and almond extract. Whisk the sugar until emulsified and smooth. Add the flour mixture, stirring just until mixed. Fold in the chocolate chips.

Scoop the batter into the prepared pan and bake in the preheated oven for about 20 minutes, or just until the brownies look fairly firm around the edges but still soft in the center. They will look slightly under-cooked, but you don't want to over-bake them. Remove the pan from the oven to a rack to cool completely.

For the glaze: In a small microwave-safe glass or ceramic bowl, combine the chocolate chips and soymilk. Heat for 30 seconds. Stir and heat for another 30 seconds. Remove from microwave and stir as needed until chocolate is melted and mixture is smooth. If necessary, heat chocolate chips for another 20 seconds or as needed. Alternatively, melt the chocolate in a double boiler. Drizzle the chocolate mixture over the cooled brownies and refrigerate until the chocolate topping is firm. Slice into brownies and serve.

Variation: For a nutty version, add about 1/2 cup toasted pecans or walnuts to the brownie batter.

Banana Breakfast Bars

It's always fun to have dessert for breakfast:

who wouldn't want to start the day with banana blondies? If it makes you
feel any better, bananas are full of potassium and flaxseed is a great source
of omega–3 fatty acids. See, you can feel good about dessert for breakfast.

**MAKES ONE
13 X 9-INCH PAN**

2 cups all-purpose flour

2 tablespoons flaxseed
  meal, preferably golden

2 teaspoons baking powder

⅛ teaspoon fine sea salt

1 cup puréed ripe bananas
  (about 2 large or 3
  medium bananas)

½ cup canola oil

½ cup granulated sugar

½ cup packed light brown
  sugar

1 cup nondairy semisweet
  chocolate chips

Preheat oven to 350°F. Grease a 13 x 9-inch glass baking dish well with shortening.

In a small bowl, whisk together the flour, flaxseed meal, baking powder, and salt.

In a large bowl, whisk together the puréed banana, oil, and both sugars. Add the flour mixture, mixing just until combined. Stir in the chocolate chips.

Spread the batter in the prepared pan, smoothing top with a spatula. Bake for 30 to 35 minutes, or until the top is golden brown and the sides are starting to pull away from pan. If you touch the center of the bars, it will leave a slight dent, and be slightly soft to the touch.

Remove to a rack to cool completely. Cut into bars once cool.

Variation: Substitute lightly toasted walnuts or pecans for the chocolate chips.

I find that a mini (or regular size) food processor works beautifully for puréeing ripe bananas. Just break the bananas into chunks and whiz them until smooth. If you have a large bunch of ripe bananas, purée them and then portion into freezer bags or containers in 1 cup measurements. This way you'll be ready to bake these bars or Banana Chocolate Chip Bread, page 26 at a moment's notice.

Lotsa Chocolate Pudding

When I'm craving something rich and chocolaty,
this little creamy number is just the ticket. One bite and I'm quickly transported
right back to childhood, enjoying a bowl of my mom's chocolate pudding.

MAKES 4 SERVINGS

- 3/4 cup granulated sugar
- 1/3 cup unsweetened cocoa powder, sifted
- 1/4 cup plus 2 tablespoons cornstarch
- 3 cups chocolate soymilk or other nondairy chocolate milk
- 1/4 cup nondairy semisweet chocolate chips
- 1 teaspoon pure vanilla extract

In a large pot, whisk together the sugar, cocoa powder, and cornstarch. Add the soymilk, whisking until smooth. Bring the mixture to a simmer over medium heat, whisking continually. If mixture looks like it's starting to scorch or burn, reduce the heat to medium low. Once the pudding comes to a simmer, lower the heat and continue simmering gently, whisking continually, for 5 to 10 minutes or until pudding is thick.

Remove the saucepan from heat and stir in the chocolate chips and vanilla, stirring until the chocolate is melted. Serve the pudding warm, or scoop into a serving bowl or individual cups. Press a piece of plastic wrap onto the surface of the pudding (to prevent a skin from forming) and refrigerate until ready to serve.

Homemade pudding makes a great lunchbox stuffer. Scoop the pudding into small lidded serving cups and refrigerate. In the morning, pop one into the lunchbox along with an ice pack. You can also freeze it in popsicle molds for a delicious frozert treat.

Chocolate Chip Bread Pudding

This is bread pudding just like your mother used to make, providing of course that your mom was vegan. This is comfort food at its very best.

MAKES ONE
8-INCH SQUARE PAN

6 to 7 cups bread cubes (a good crusty rustic bread or French baguette is great)

1 (14-ounce) can light coconut milk

1 1/2 cups plain unsweetened almond milk

1/2 cup plus 2 tablespoons granulated sugar

3 tablespoons tapioca or cornstarch

1/2 cup nondairy semisweet chocolate chips

Preheat the oven to 350°F. Grease an 8-inch square glass baking dish with shortening.

Place the bread in a large bowl. Pour coconut milk over bread. In a medium bowl or large measuring cup, whisk together the almond milk, sugar, and tapioca starch until starch is well mixed and there aren't any lumps. The sugar may not completely dissolve, but that's okay. Pour almond milk mixture over bread cubes and coconut milk, mixing well. Let bread mixture sit for about 15 minutes, or until bread is soft and has absorbed most of the milk. Scoop mixture into prepared baking dish. Sprinkle top with chocolate chips, lightly pressing some of them in bread mixture.

Bake pudding in preheated oven for about 45 to 50 minutes, or until puffed, slightly golden, firm to the touch and the milk has been absorbed. Remove from the oven. Let cool down slightly before serving. Serve warm or refrigerate cooled pudding until ready to serve.

Pineapple Coconut Cups

This creamy tropical dessert is very pudding-like.

It tastes rich, but is very light and refreshing. If you prefer your
desserts a little sweeter, add the full 4 tablespoons of sugar.

MAKES 4 SERVINGS

3 cups unsweetened
   pineapple juice

1 cup light coconut milk

2 to 4 tablespoons
   granulated sugar

2 teaspoons agar powder

4 teaspoons cornstarch

4 teaspoons water

In a saucepan, combine pineapple juice, coconut milk,
sugar, and agar powder, until everything is blended. Let
the mixture sit for a full 5 minutes so that the agar can
soften.

Place saucepan over medium heat and bring to a simmer, whisking occasionally. Let simmer for 2 minutes to
completely dissolve agar.

In a small bowl, whisk together cornstarch and water
until smooth. Whisk into hot pineapple mixture.

Pour hot juice mixture into 4 glass bowls or parfait
cups. Let cool for 15 minutes on counter and then
refrigerate for several hours before serving.

Variation: If you want fruit in your dessert, once juice
mixture is halfway thickened, stir in drained canned
pineapple tidbits.

Agar powder is a wonderful ingredient to keep on hand
for jelling recipes. It's 100% vegetarian and made from seaweed (although it's flavorless). Look for agar powder in
Asian markets and online. Agar flakes will not work here
like agar powder will.

Cranberry Orange Cups

Inspired by the parfait glasses of Jell-o that I remember from many diners as a kid, this version is made with an orange and cranberry juice combo, and lightly gelled with agar. If you prefer your gel sweeter, add the full 2 tablespoons of sugar.

MAKES 2 TO 4 SERVINGS

1 cup fresh orange juice

1 cup cranberry juice cocktail

1 to 2 tablespoons granulated sugar

1 teaspoon agar powder

In a saucepan, whisk together the orange juice, cranberry juice, sugar, and agar powder, until everything is well mixed. Let the mixture sit for a full 5 minutes so that the agar can soften.

Place the saucepan over medium heat and bring to a simmer, whisking occasionally. Let simmer for a full 2 minutes to completely dissolve the agar, whisking periodically. Remove from the heat. Pour the hot juice mixture into small glass cups, bowls, or parfait cups. Let cool for 20 minutes and then refrigerate for several hours, or until completely firm, before serving.

Variation: If you want fruit in your gel, once the juice mixture is halfway thickened, stir in fresh grapes or canned Mandarin oranges.

This recipe comes out best when it's made with a sweetened cranberry juice cocktail. Look for agar powder in Asian markets and online. Agar flakes will not work here.

Old–Fashioned Rice Pudding

When my kids were young, I used to make them rice pudding
for breakfast. They both had a hard time with their "r's" when they spoke, so instead of calling it rice
pudding, they would call it "wice pubbin." Many years later, we still refer to it as wice pubbin.

MAKES 4 TO 6 SERVINGS

1 cup medium-grain sushi
rice (such as calrose)

1/2 cup raisins, optional

1 1/2 to 2 cups soymilk or
almond milk (plain or
vanilla), or as needed

1/2 cup granulated sugar

1 teaspoon pure vanilla
extract

Freshly ground cinnamon

In a large saucepan over medium heat, combine 2 cups
water, rice, and raisins (if using), and bring to a boil.
Reduce heat to low, cover, and simmer for 15 minutes.
Remove saucepan from heat and let sit, covered, for 5
minutes. Remove the cover.

Add 1 cup of the soymilk and the sugar to the cooked
rice, stirring until combined. Return the saucepan to
stove. Cook over medium heat, stirring often. Continue
adding more milk as the pudding cooks and thickens,
stirring as needed. Cook for 15 to 20 minutes, or until
the pudding is very thick and creamy. If the pudding is
too thick, stir in a little more soymilk as needed to thin
slightly. Remove the saucepan from the heat and stir in
the vanilla. Scoop the pudding into serving dishes and
sprinkle with ground cinnamon. Refrigerate pudding
until ready to serve.

Variation: Rice pudding naturally lends itself to many
different flavor combinations. Although the traditional
diner-style is vanilla with cinnamon, try playing around
with different variations. Here are some of my favorites: A
sprinkle of freshly ground nutmeg adds a sweet eggnog
flavor, a dash of almond extract (and a garnish of toasted
almonds) gives the pudding a lovely almond flavor, dried
cherries instead of the raisins gives it a more modern edge,
and chopped candied ginger adds some zing.

All-Purpose Pastry Dough

Although not everyone wants to make their pie crusts
from scratch, there is nothing quite like homemade. This recipe is from my book
The Complete Book of Pies (Robert Rose, 2008), and is super easy to make.
I like to use the food processor, which makes it go together quickly.

MAKES ONE 9-INCH SINGLE CRUST

1½ cups all-purpose flour

1 tablespoon confectioners' sugar

¼ teaspoon fine sea salt

½ cup very cold vegetable shortening, cut into pieces or small chunks

3 to 5 tablespoons ice cold water

In a food processor, combine the flour, sugar, and salt, pulsing until mixed. Add the shortening, pulsing again until the mixture resembles coarse meal.

Add 3 tablespoons of the ice water to the flour mixture, pulsing until moist clumps start to form. Stop to test the dough by pressing together with your fingertips to see if it's moist enough to hold together. You don't want it too wet. If the dough is too dry, add 1 to 2 tablespoons more ice water as needed. Remove the blade and gather the dough together into a ball, flattening it into a disc. Wrap it in plastic wrap and refrigerate for 20 to 30 minutes.

On a lightly floured surface, roll out the dough into a circle large enough to fit your pie plate (plus an extra inch or so), lightly dusting the work surface and dough as necessary to keep the dough from sticking. You can also roll the dough out on a silicone baking or rolling mat or between 2 pieces of parchment paper. Press the dough into a lightly greased pie plate, trimming the dough evenly along the edge, leaving about a ½-inch overhang. Pinch the overhang to form a decorative edge. Prick the crust in several places with a fork. Place the pie plate in the freezer for 1 hour or until it's cold and firm.

To partially bake the crust: preheat the oven to 375°F.

Line the chilled crust with parchment paper or foil (fold in half, then shape into a bowl shape) and a layer of dried beans or pie weights to weigh it down. Bake for 20 to 25 minutes or until the shell is golden brown and the bottom is no longer moist. Keep an eye on your shell as it's baking (preferably without opening the oven too much) and look for visual signs of doneness. If you use a glass pie plate, you can look at the bottom to check that all of the moisture has baked out of the crust.

To fully bake the crust: preheat the oven to 375°F.

Line the chilled crust with parchment paper or foil (fold it in half, then shape into a bowl shape) and a layer of dried beans or pie weights to weigh it down. Bake for 20 to 25 minutes or until the shell is golden brown and the bottom is no longer moist. If you use a glass pie plate, you can look at the bottom to check that all of the moisture has baked out of the crust. Carefully remove the paper and weights. Return the crust to the oven and bake for 5 minutes more or just until lightly browned.

Tip: For a very tender crust, make sure not to over-blend the dough in the food processor. I also like to keep little baggies with pre-measured shortening in my freezer (labeled, of course), so that I can make pie crust at a moment's notice.

Apple Crumb Pie

What could be more American than apple pie?

Being a pie fanatic myself, I just had to share one of my favorite apple pie recipes. Try serving the pie à la mode with a scoop of homemade vanilla ice cream (see page 152). Don't worry if you don't have time to make a pie crust from scratch. A good-quality frozen crust is perfectly acceptable.

 MAKES ONE 9-INCH PIE

Filling

5 large Granny Smith apples, peeled, cored and thinly sliced

³/₄ cup packed light brown sugar

2 tablespoons unbleached all-purpose flour

2 teaspoons lemon zest

1 teaspoon ground cinnamon

1 (9-inch) frozen vegan deep-dish pie crust (leave in the freezer until ready to use) or homemade crust (see page 136)

Topping

³/₄ cup unbleached all-purpose flour

¹/₂ cup packed light brown sugar

¹/₂ teaspoon ground cinnamon

4 tablespoons (¹/₂ stick) non-hydrogenated vegan margarine, melted

Preheat the oven to 400°F.

For the filling: In a large bowl, mix together the apples, brown sugar, flour, lemon zest, and cinnamon. Make sure that the apples are well coated.

Scoop the filling into the frozen crust. Gently press the apples into the crust. Bake the pie in the preheated oven and bake for 40 minutes.

For the topping: In a small bowl, stir together the flour, brown sugar, and cinnamon until well mixed. Add the melted margarine and stir until mixed. Using your hands, squeeze the topping so that it forms crumbly pieces.

Remove the pie from the oven and reduce the temperature to 350°F. Crumble the topping over the apples. Bake the pie for another 20 to 30 minutes, or until the topping is lightly browned. If the pie starts to brown too quickly, loosely place a piece of foil over the pie, tenting it, and continue baking.

Let the pie cool completely before serving.

Tip: Look for frozen organic vegan piecrusts at well stocked grocery and health food stores (see Resources page 183). If your apples aren't really large, use 6 or 7, depending on the size.

Variations: Omit the lemon zest and add 1 teaspoon ground allspice and ¹/₂ teaspoon ground nutmeg. For an apple raisin pie, omit the lemon zest and add ¹/₃ to ¹/₂ cup raisins to the filling. For an apple cranberry pie, use 3 apples for the filling and add 1 cup fresh or frozen cranberries.

Banana Pudding Pie

Here is my tribute to the old Southern favorite, banana pudding. I've given it a little modern twist and put the pudding over a vanilla cookie crust with a layer of fresh sliced bananas. Vegan pudding has never tasted so good!

MAKES 6 TO 8 SERVINGS

Crust

21 vegan cream-filled vanilla sandwich cookies

4 tablespoons $1/2$ stick non-hydrogenated vegan margarine, melted

Filling

2 small bananas, sliced

$1/2$ cup cornstarch (not packed)

2 cups vanilla soymilk, divided

$3/4$ cup soy creamer

1 cup granulated sugar

1 tablespoon non-hydrogenated vegan margarine

1 teaspoon pure vanilla extract or paste

Preheat oven to 350°F. Grease a 9-inch glass pie plate with shortening.

For the crust: In a food processor, pulse the cookies into fine crumbs. Add the melted margarine and pulse again until incorporated and mixed well. Press the crumbs into the prepared pie plate. Place the crust in the oven and bake until fragrant, about 10 minutes. Remove crust from the oven and let cool completely on a rack.

For the filling: Place the banana slices into the bottom of the cooled crust, spreading them into an even layer.

In a small bowl, whisk together the cornstarch and $1/2$ cup of the soymilk. Set aside.

In a medium saucepan, combine the remaining soymilk, creamer, and sugar, stirring well. Place the saucepan over medium heat, whisking continuously, and bring to a simmer. Give the reserved cornstarch mixture a stir to mix, and add to the hot soymilk. Whisk the pudding continuously, about 5 minutes, until the mixture is very thick. Remove from the heat and whisk in the margarine and vanilla. Scoop the pudding into a bowl and place the bowl in a larger shallow bowl filled part way with ice water. Whisk the pudding continuously for the first 5 minutes or so as it cools, then whisk intermittently for another 10 minutes or so. Whisk it as it cools to prevent a skin from forming on the top.

Once the pudding is no longer hot, and just a little warm, spread the pudding into the crust over the bananas, swirling the top slightly with the back of a spoon. Refrigerate the pie for a couple of hours, or until the pudding has firmed up enough to slice.

Double Chocolate Strawberry Pie

This pie takes dessert to a whole new level,

and will have everyone asking you what fancy bakery it came from. It goes together easily, requiring very little cooking. It's a fun twist on the traditional diner–style strawberry pie, with layers of chocolate cream and fresh seasonal berries.

MAKES ONE 9-INCH PIE

Crust

- 21 vegan cream-filled chocolate sandwich cookies (or substitute vanilla sandwich cookies)
- 4 tablespoons ($^{1}/_{2}$ stick) non-hydrogenated vegan margarine, melted

Filling

- $^{3}/_{4}$ cup dairy-free semi-sweet chocolate chips
- $^{1}/_{4}$ cup vanilla soymilk
- 1 tablespoon strawberry or raspberry liqueur
- 4 cups fresh strawberries, rinsed and hulled and patted dry

Topping

- $^{1}/_{2}$ cup dairy-free semisweet chocolate chips
- 1 tablespoon vanilla soymilk
- 1 tablespoon strawberry or raspberry liqueur

Preheat oven to 350°F. Grease a 9-inch glass pie plate For the crust: In a food processor, pulse cookies until you've got crumbs. Add the melted margarine and pulse again until incorporated and mixed well. Press crumbs into the prepared pie plate. Place the crust in the oven and bake until fragrant, about 10 minutes. Remove crust from the oven and let cool completely on a rack.

For the filling: In a small microwave-safe glass or ceramic bowl, combine the chocolate chips, soymilk, and liqueur. Heat for 30 seconds. Stir and heat for another 30 seconds. Remove from microwave and stir as needed until chocolate is melted and mixture is smooth. If necessary, heat chocolate chips for another 20 seconds or as needed. Alternatively, melt the chocolate in a double boiler.

Spread the smooth chocolate mixture into the bottom of the chocolate crust. Top with whole strawberries, arranging them with the tips up to cover the chocolate filling entirely. Gently press the strawberries into the chocolate crust, with a very light touch.

For the topping: In a small microwave-safe glass or ceramic bowl, combine the chocolate chips, soymilk, and the liqueur. Heat is the microwave in 20-second intervals, stirring until chocolate is melted and mixture is smooth and shiny. Alternatively, melt the chocolate in a double boiler. Drizzle the warm topping over the pie in a decorative fashion.Refrigerate the pie for one hour, or until the chocolate is firm.

Tip: This pie is best served the day it is made.

Pineapple Coconut Cream Pie

When I close my eyes and think of diner desserts, cream pies
are the first thing to come to mind. Silken tofu gives the filling a nice boost of protein,
and contributes to its silky texture. The coconut milk adds richness and tropical flavor.

MAKES ONE 9-INCH PIE

Crust

**1½ cups graham
cracker crumbs**

**¼ cup packed light
brown sugar**

**4 tablespoons (½ stick)
non-hydrogenated vegan
margarine, melted**

Filling

**1 (12.3-ounce) package
extra firm silken tofu**

**¾ cup coconut milk
(not low-fat)**

¾ cup granulated sugar

2 tablespoons cornstarch

**¾ cup canned crushed
pineapple in juice,
undrained**

Preheat oven to 350°F. Grease a 9-inch glass pie plate.
For the crust: In the bowl of a food processor, pulse the
graham crackers and brown sugar until finely ground.
Add the melted margarine, and pulse until well mixed.
Scoop the crumbs into the prepared pie plate, pressing
into the bottom and up sides of the pan. Place the crust
in the oven and bake until fragrant and edges are lightly
golden, about 10 minutes. Remove the crust from the
oven and let cool completely on a rack.

For the filling: In a clean food processor bowl, combine
the tofu and coconut milk and blend until ultra-smooth.
This might take a few minutes, as you don't want any
lumps of tofu. Add the sugar and cornstarch, blending
again until very smooth.

Place the coconut mixture into a medium saucepan
and stir in the pineapple. Over medium heat, bring the
mixture to a simmer, whisking continuously until thick
and custardy, about 5 to 10 minutes. Adjust the heat as
necessary so that the filling does not burn.

Scoop the hot coconut mixture into prepared pie
shell, smoothing top. Let the pie cool to room temperature and then refrigerate for several hours or overnight.
Serve the pie chilled.

Silken tofu is a magical ingredient for so many recipes. Part
of the beauty lies in the fact that once silken tofu is whipped
up in the blender or food processor, it becomes super silky and
smooth. Mori-Nu carries a line of shelf-stable (non-refriger-
ated) silken tofu, perfect to keep in the pantry for last-minute
cream pie cravings.

Chocolate Mint Truffle Pie

This pie is where Girl Scout Thin Mint Cookies and chocolate mousse meet. It also happens to be a show–stopper dessert, making the perfect dessert to serve to guests if you want them to say, "Wow, there is no way that that pie is vegan."

MAKES ONE 9-INCH PIE

Crust

21 vegan cream-filled chocolate sandwich cookies (or substitute vanilla sandwich cookies)

4 tablespoons (1/2 stick) non-hydrogenated vegan margarine, melted

Filling

2 cups dairy-free semisweet chocolate chips

1/4 cup vanilla soymilk

1 1/2 boxes (12.3 ounces per box) silken firm or extra firm tofu, at room temperature

1/2 cup confectioners' sugar

1/2 teaspoon peppermint extract

Preheat oven to 350°F. Grease a 9-inch glass pie.

For the crust: In a food processor, pulse the cookies until they are fine crumbs. Add the melted butter and pulse again until incorporated and mixed well. Press the crumbs into the prepared pie plate. Place the crust in the oven and bake until fragrant, about 10 minutes. Remove from the oven and let cool completely on a rack.

For the filling: in a microwave-safe bowl, combine the chocolate chips and soymilk and heat on high for 30 seconds. Give the chocolate a stir and heat for another 30 seconds. Stir until the chocolate is completely melted, smooth, and shiny. If the chocolate is not completely melted after stirring, heat for another 15 to 20 seconds. Alternatively you can melt the chocolate in a double boiler.

In the bowl of a food processor, add the tofu and blend until smooth. Add the melted chocolate, and blend again until it is ultra smooth. Add the confectioners' sugar and peppermint extract and blend again until mixture is smooth and fluffy.

Spread the chocolate mixture into cooled piecrust and refrigerate for several hours or overnight, until the pie is firm enough to slice. If desired, top with coarsely crushed sandwich cookies or chocolate chips.

Tip: Although you can melt chocolate in a double boiler using a metal bowl set atop a pot of gently simmering water, I actually prefer melting chocolate in a microwave. It really just comes down to pure laziness on my part, but it's quick, easy, and only uses one bowl.

Easy Blackberry Skillet Pie

I always have a couple of dessert recipes in my "bag of tricks,"
the recipes that I reach for when I have to throw a fabulous dessert together quickly for drop-in guests. This pie never disappoints, and because it's crust-less and you can use frozen berries on hand, you can literally make it in no time flat. No matter how easy it is to make, your guests will be impressed with your pie-making skills. Guaranteed!

MAKES ONE 10-INCH PIE

Filling
- **6 cups frozen blackberries**
- **²/₃ cup granulated sugar**
- **¹/₄ cup cornstarch**

Topping
- **³/₄ cup unbleached all-purpose flour**
- **¹/₂ cup old fashioned rolled oats**
- **¹/₂ cup packed light brown sugar**
- **1 teaspoon ground cinnamon**
- **4 tablespoons (¹/₂ stick) non-hydrogenated vegan margarine, melted**

Preheat oven to 400°F. Grease a 10-inch cast-iron or ovenproof skillet or glass or ceramic pie plate with shortening.

For the filling: In a saucepan, combine the blackberries, sugar, and ¹/₄ cup water. Bring mixture to a simmer over medium heat, stirring occasionally.

In a small bowl, whisk together cornstarch and 5 tablespoons water until smooth. Stir the cornstarch mixture into the hot berries, and simmer until thick and mixture is clear, stirring continuously.

Remove the saucepan from the heat and scoop the berry mixture into the prepared pan.

For the topping: In a small bowl, mix together the flour, oats, brown sugar, and cinnamon. Add the melted margarine, stirring until incorporated. Using your fingertips, work the margarine into the flour mixture, squeezing until nice and crumbly.

Sprinkle the topping over the blackberry filling and bake in preheated oven for about 20 minutes, or until the topping is nicely browned.

Variation: Use frozen boysenberries, blueberries, or mixed berries for different berry pie combinations.

Chocolate Chip Skillet Pie

I love serving desserts in cast–iron skillets.

The pie is delicious served à la mode, with a scoop of
homemade (or store–bought, if you must) ice cream.

MAKES ONE 10-INCH PIE

1¹/₂ cups unbleached
  all-purpose flour

¹/₂ teaspoon baking powder

1 tablespoon flaxseed meal,
  preferably golden

3 tablespoons hot water

1¹/₄ cups packed light
  brown sugar

¹/₂ cup (1 stick) non-hydrogenated vegan margarine,
  softened

1 teaspoon pure vanilla
  extract

1 cup dairy-free semisweet
  chocolate chips

¹/₂ cup lightly toasted
  pecans

Preheat oven to 350°F. Grease a 10-inch cast-iron or oven-proof skillet with shortening.

In a small bowl, combine the flour and baking powder. In a very small bowl, mix together the ground flaxseed and hot water. Set aside to thicken slightly.

In a large bowl, cream together the brown sugar and margarine until light and fluffy. Add the flaxseed mixture, beating until smooth. Add the vanilla, and beat until well incorporated. Add the flour mixture, beating just until the batter comes together. Don't over mix. Stir in the chocolate chips and pecans.

Spread mixture into the prepared pan, and bake in the preheated oven for 30 to 40 minutes, or until puffed and golden brown. When the top of the pie is lightly touched, it should only leave a little indentation.

Remove the skillet from the oven to a rack, and let cool for 15 minutes.

Tip: Serve this cookie pie warm, with a scoop of home-made peanut butter chocolate chunk ice cream (see page 153).

Almond Raspberry Cake

This is a scrumptious cake, perfect for special occasions

or for afternoon tea. I go crazy for almonds and raspberries, especially when they're combined together in a delicate and tender cake. This cake won't let you down!

MAKES ONE
8-INCH CAKE

Cake

2 cups cake flour, sifted

1 cup granulated sugar

1 tablespoon baking powder

$1/8$ teaspoon fine sea salt

1 cup plus 1 tablespoon plain almond or rice milk, divided

$1/3$ cup canola oil

1 teaspoon pure vanilla extract

1 teaspoon almond extract

$1/2$ pint basket fresh raspberries (about $1 1/4$ cups)

Frosting

9 ounces (about 2 cups) confectioners' sugar

3 tablespoons non-hydrogenated vegan margarine, softened

2 tablespoons plain soymilk or almond milk, or as needed to make a fluffy frosting

$1/4$ teaspoon pure almond extract

Preheat oven to 350°F. Grease an 8 inch-square glass baking dish with shortening.

For the cake: In a small bowl, whisk together the flour, sugar, baking powder, and salt.

In a large bowl, whisk together half of the almond milk, oil, and vanilla and almond extracts. Whisk in half of the flour mixture. Add the remaining almond milk alternately with the remaining flour mixture. Add the flour mixture, whisking just until smooth. Don't over mix.

Scoop the batter into the prepared pan. Sprinkle the raspberries over the top of the cake. Bake for 45 to 50 minutes, or until a tester inserted into the center comes out clean.

For the frosting: While the cake is cooling, prepare the frosting. In a medium bowl with a hand mixer or stand mixer, beat together the confectioners' sugar, margarine, soymilk, and the almond extract. Beat the frosting until light and fluffy. If necessary, add another $1/2$ tablespoon of milk to make a soft and spreadable frosting. Using an offset spatula or the back of a large spoon, spread the frosting over the top of the cooled cake.

Tip: Substitute frozen (not thawed) raspberries for the fresh berries. The frozen berries will sink down into the cake a little more than will fresh berries.

Lemon Diner Cheesecake

This New York–style cheesecake has a wonderfully creamy
delicate taste of lemon zest. Try it unadorned, or with a fresh fruit topping. I have heard many people
exclaim that this cheesecake must be made with dairy, because it's just too creamy and delicious.

MAKES ONE
9¹/₂-INCH PIE

Crust

2 cups cookie crumbs (I use
   animal crackers), about 9
   ounces

6 tablespoons non-hydro-
   genated vegan margarine,
   melted and cooled

Filling

2 (8-ounce) tubs soy cream
   cheese

1 (12-ounce) box firm or
   extra-firm silken tofu

1 cup granulated sugar

4 tablespoons fresh lemon
   juice

Zest of 1¹/₂ lemons

2 tablespoons cornstarch

Preheat the oven to 350°F. Grease a 9¹/₂-inch deep-dish
glass pie plate with shortening.

For the crust: In a large bowl, mix together the cookie
crumbs and melted margarine. Press onto the bottom
and sides of the prepared pie plate. Set aside.

For the filling: In the bowl of a food processor fitted
with the metal blade, combine cream cheese, tofu,
sugar, lemon juice, zest, and cornstarch. Process until
the mixture is ultra-smooth, about 1 minute.

   Pour the cheesecake mixture into the prepared
cookie crust. Place in the middle of the preheated oven
and bake for 40 to 45 minutes, or until just lightly
golden.

   Remove the pie to a rack to cool completely before
refrigerating overnight. Once the pie has had a chance
to firm up overnight, slice and serve.

Tip: This uses a slightly larger pie plate than the other pie
recipes in this book.

Look for Tofutti soy cream cheese and Mori–Nu silken
tofu in well-stocked grocery and health food stores. These
are two brands that work well, and I use often.

Chocolate Cherry Cake

When I was young, I was completely mesmerized by black forest cakes. There was just something about the way the chocolate, cherries, and cream all danced together into one glorious cake. This cake is my little nod to the old Black Forest bakery cakes. It's got a totally different look, but the decadent flavors of chocolate and cherry remain.

MAKES ONE 8-INCH SQUARE CAKE

Cake

- 1½ cups unbleached all-purpose flour
- ½ cup unsweetened Dutch process cocoa powder
- 2 teaspoons baking powder
- ½ teaspoon baking soda
- ⅛ teaspoon fine sea salt
- 1 cup packed light brown sugar
- ¼ cup granulated sugar
- ½ cup vanilla soymilk or almond milk or rice milk, divided
- ⅓ cup canola oil
- 3 tablespoons red wine, rum, or cherry liqueur
- 2 teaspoons pure vanilla extract
- ½ teaspoon pure almond extract
- 1 cup canned cherry pie filling (not cherries in juice)
- ½ cup dairy-free semisweet chocolate chips

Topping

- ¾ cup dairy-free semi-sweet chocolate chips
- ¼ cup vanilla soymilk
- 1 tablespoon dark rum or cherry liqueur, optional

Preheat the oven to 350°F. Grease an 8-inch square glass baking dish with shortening.

For the cake: In a small bowl, whisk together the flour, cocoa powder, baking powder, baking soda, and salt. In a large bowl, whisk together the brown sugar, granulated sugar, half of the soymilk, oil, red wine, vanilla and almond extracts. Whisk mixture until smooth. Add the flour mixture, followed by the remaining soymilk, whisking or stirring just until mixed and smooth. Gently stir in the cherry pie filling. Don't over mix.

Scoop the batter into the prepared pan. Sprinkle the chocolate chips over the top. Bake the cake in the preheated oven for 45 to 50 minutes, or until a tester inserted in center comes out clean and the top of the cake springs back when lightly touched.

Let cake cool completely on a rack.

For the topping: While the cake is cooling, in a small microwave-safe glass or ceramic bowl, combine the chocolate chips, soymilk, and rum. Heat for 20 seconds. Stir and heat for another 20 seconds. Remove from microwave and stir as needed until chocolate is melted and mixture is smooth and shiny. Alternatively, you can melt the chocolate in a double boiler. Spread the warm chocolate mixture evenly over the top of the cake, using an offset spatula or the back of a spoon. Refrigerate the cake for an hour or so to let the chocolate firm up. Once the chocolate is firm, take the cake out of the refrigerator and serve.

Dark Chocolate Chunk Ice Cream

This ice cream is the stuff that vegan dreams are made of.

It took me a while to get a perfect dairy-free ice cream, but here you have it.
The deep intense chocolate flavor will satisfy those die-hard chocolate fans.

MAKES ABOUT 2½ PINTS

1 cup non-dairy semisweet chocolate chips

2½ cups vanilla soymilk (not low- or non-fat), chilled

½ cup coconut milk (not light)

½ cup Dutch process cocoa powder, sifted

⅔ cup granulated sugar

4 teaspoons pure vanilla extract

¼ teaspoon xanthan gum

Place the chocolate in a microwave-safe dish and heat on high for 30 seconds. Stir, and if chocolate is not almost melted, heat for another 30 seconds or as needed. When chocolate is almost melted, stir gently and chocolate should melt the rest of the way from the heat of the bowl. Don't overheat the chocolate or it will burn and turn gritty. Alternatively, you can melt the chocolate in a double boiler.

In a blender jar, combine the soymilk, coconut milk, melted chocolate, cocoa powder, sugar, and vanilla. Blend until the mixture is ultra-smooth. Add the xanthan gum and blend again until smooth.

Pour the ice cream mixture into an ice cream maker and freeze according to the manufacturer's directions.

Serve the ice cream right away or transfer to an airtight container and freeze until ready to serve.

Tip: This ice cream is best served the day that it is made. Even if xanthan gum is something that you don't have in your pantry, track it down. The xanthan gum helps create the magic in these ice cream recipes.

Variation: Add some fun goodies into the ice cream when it's almost done freezing. Try chopped toasted almonds, brownie pieces, or even chocolate sandwich cookies.

Very Vanilla Ice Cream

This is a silky and delicious ice cream, full of rich vanilla flavor.
Who would have thought that dairy-free ice cream could taste so good? I like to think of this as the ultimate topper for a piece of pie or layered into a sundae, though there's no need to stop there. Imagine this ice cream affogato-style with a shot of espresso, or blended into a malt. Whoa!

MAKES ABOUT 1 QUART

2$\frac{1}{2}$ cups vanilla soymilk, (not low- or non-fat), chilled

1 cup coconut milk (not light)

$\frac{2}{3}$ cup granulated sugar

1$\frac{1}{2}$ tablespoons pure vanilla paste or extract

$\frac{1}{4}$ teaspoon xanthan gum

In a blender jar, combine the soymilk, coconut milk, sugar, and vanilla. Blend until the mixture is ultra-smooth. Add the xanthan gum and blend again until smooth.

Pour the ice cream mixture into an ice cream maker and freeze according to the manufacturer's directions.

Serve the ice cream right away or transfer to an airtight container and freeze until ready to serve.

Tip: Homemade ice cream will come out of the ice cream maker fairly soft, similar in texture to soft-serve ice cream. If you want the consistency of the ice cream to be firmer, pack the ice cream into an airtight container and freeze it for a couple of hours. Personally, I find the soft frozen texture to be silky and very gelato-like.

Variations: There are many different ways that you can embellish this ice cream. For a mint chip version, add 1$\frac{1}{2}$ teaspoons peppermint extract for the vanilla and $\frac{1}{2}$ cup miniature chocolate chips at the end. Add broken chocolate sandwich cookies for a cookies-and-cream variation (added near the end of freezing) or $\frac{1}{2}$ cup or so of rum-soaked raisins (drained) for a rum raisin version. Fresh berries or chopped and peeled fresh peaches or nectarines are fantastic, too. The sky's the limit!

Peanut Butter Chocolate Chunk Ice Cream

Chocolate and peanut butter are the original dynamic duo,
and I can't imagine one without the other. Here I've joined the two together, into a smooth
and creamy ice cream, which will keep your taste buds screaming for more!

MAKES ABOUT 1 QUART

1¹/₂ cups vanilla soymilk
(not low- or non-fat),
chilled

¹/₂ cup soy creamer, chilled

¹/₂ cup natural peanut
butter

¹/₂ cup lightly packed light
brown sugar

1 teaspoon pure vanilla
extract

¹/₄ teaspoon xanthan gum

4 ounces dairy-free semi-
sweet or dark chocolate,
chopped

In a blender jar, combine the soymilk, soy creamer, peanut butter, brown sugar, and vanilla. Blend until the mixture is ultra smooth. Add the xanthan gum, and blend again until smooth.

Pour the peanut butter mixture into an ice cream maker and freeze according to the manufacturer's directions.

While the ice cream is freezing, place the chocolate in a microwave-safe dish and heat on high for 30 seconds. Stir, and if chocolate is not almost melted, heat for another 30 seconds or as needed. When the chocolate is almost melted, stir gently and the chocolate should melt the rest of the way from the heat of the bowl. Don't over-heat the chocolate or it will burn and turn gritty. Alterna-tively, you can melt the chocolate in a double boiler.

When the ice cream is thick and almost done, slowly drizzle the melted chocolate through the hole in the top of the ice cream machine, in a thick and steady stream. As the ice cream freezes, the chocolate will firm up into chunks. Remove the ice cream from the machine and stir a bit, to break up the large pieces of chocolate.

Serve right away or transfer to an airtight container and freeze until ready to serve.

Homemade vegan ice cream is super easy to make. Of course there's a little equipment involved, but that goes without saying. A good ice cream maker can be found for about $50, and sometimes even less than that. I love to make ice cream year–round, since nothing beats the flavor and texture of homemade.

Tip: If your ice cream maker doesn't have a pouring hole in the top, you can still make the chocolate chunks. Scoop about a third of the finished ice cream into a storage container and drizzle a third of the chocolate over the top. Use a spatula to swirl the chocolate through the ice cream, and repeat with more layers of ice cream and chocolate, making sure the chocolate swirl gets all the way through the ice cream. Freeze until ready to serve.

Mocha Malt

Malts and diners go together like Fred and Ginger.
Personally, I think that a malt is best enjoyed alongside a veggie burger,
although it's just as delicious for dessert.

 MAKES 2 SERVINGS

**2 cups store-bought vegan
    mocha swirl or coffee
    ice cream**

$^1/_2$ to $^3/_4$ cup vanilla soymilk

**$^1/_3$ cup dairy-free malt
    powder**

**1 tablespoon instant
    coffee, optional**

In a blender, add the ice cream, $^1/_2$ cup soymilk, malt powder, and instant coffee if using. Blend until smooth. If the blender seems to be bogging down a bit, you may need to add another 2 to 4 tablespoons of soymilk. Start with the smaller amount, as you want the malt to be thick, not runny.

Pour the malt into glasses and serve right away.

Variations: For a vanilla malt, use vanilla ice cream in place of the mocha swirl, and a teaspoon of vanilla paste or extract. For a chocolate version, use chocolate ice cream and a drizzle of dairy-free chocolate syrup. You can also make a cherry chocolate malted, substituting cherry chocolate chip ice cream for the mocha swirl. In other words, let your imagination go wild!

Tip: You can make this with homemade ice cream; just make sure it's pretty well frozen first. Regular malt powder that you find in the grocery store contains dairy. Look for powdered malt extract, which is a non-diastatic barley malt, and is made from the evaporated concentrate of bar-ley malt (check the packaging for the correct variety). The malt extract can also be used as a natural sweetener. Look for it in natural foods stores and online.

Sauces & Incidentals

Agave Maple Syrup

This syrup is a delicious blend of buttery agave nectar
and pure maple syrup. With the rising cost of pure maple syrup, this is a more
economical pancake topping that's even better than the original, if I do say so myself.

MAKES ABOUT 1 CUP

¹/₂ cup agave nectar

¹/₂ cup pure maple syrup

³/₄ teaspoon pure maple
   extract

In a small saucepan, combine the agave and maple
syrup, stirring until combined. Warm the maple mixture
over medium-high heat, stirring occasionally, just until
warm.

  Remove the saucepan from the heat and stir in the
maple extract. Let the syrup cool completely. Store the
syrup in a covered bottle or jar in the refrigerator.

Look for agave nectar in grocery and natural food stores.
Both the light and dark varieties will work in this recipe.

Strawberry Sauce

Homemade strawberry sauce is fantastic on waffles and pancakes or drizzled over cheesecake. It always brings me back to the days when my grandmother would take me out for breakfast at her local pancake house. I would always order the strawberry waffles.

MAKES ABOUT 2¹/₃ CUPS

1 pound frozen strawberries, thawed

¹/₂ cup granulated sugar, or to taste

2 tablespoons cornstarch

In a medium saucepan, mix together the strawberries, sugar, and ¹/₂ cup of water. Bring to a simmer over medium heat, stirring occasionally.

In a small bowl, mix together cornstarch and 2 tablespoons of water until smooth. Add the cornstarch mixture into the simmering strawberries, stirring well. Continue stirring and cooking the sauce until it is thickened and glossy. Remove from the heat and serve warm.

Creamy Sage and Pepper Gravy

This is the gravy that I love to serve on biscuits,

for the ultimate in comfort food breakfasts. Depending on your group and what you're serving this gravy with, you may want to double the recipe. Trust me when I say this.

MAKES ABOUT 2 CUPS

- ¼ cup unbleached all-purpose flour
- 3 tablespoons nutritional yeast flakes
- 2 cups plain unsweetened soymilk, plus more as needed
- 1 teaspoon dried rubbed sage
- 1 teaspoon granulated onion
- 1 teaspoon fine sea salt, or to taste
- 1 teaspoon freshly cracked black pepper, to taste
- ¼ teaspoon ground white pepper, or to taste
- 1 tablespoon non-hydrogenated vegan margarine, softened

In a large saucepan, whisk together the flour and nutritional yeast flakes. Whisk in the soymilk, until the mixture is very smooth. Alternatively, use a hand or immersion blender and blend until smooth. Whisk in the sage and granulated onion. Add the salt, and white and black peppers to taste.

Place the saucepan over medium heat and, whisking continuously, bring to a simmer. Whisk in margarine. Reduce the heat to medium-low, and continue whisking and cooking until the gravy is thickened and smooth. Adjust seasonings to taste, adding more soymilk to thin as needed.

Serve the gravy hot.

Garlic Dill Sauce

This silky sauce is perfect for drizzling over your homemade breakfasts, especially for the Breakfast Benedicts Florentine (see page 48) as an alternative to Hollandaise sauce. Not only is it creamy and flavorful, but it has none of the saturated fat that you'd find in traditional Hollandaise. Feel free to make this a day ahead, so that your Benedicts go together in a jiffy!

MAKES ABOUT 2 CUPS

- 1 (12-ounce) package silken tofu
- 4½ tablespoons freshly squeezed lemon juice
- 4 teaspoons Dijon mustard
- 3 tablespoons extra-virgin olive oil
- 2 tablespoon nutritional yeast flakes
- 2 cloves garlic, pressed or minced
- 1 tablespoon fresh dill or 1 teaspoon dried
- ¾ teaspoon fine sea salt, or to taste
- ¾ teaspoon granulated onion
- ¼ teaspoon ground turmeric
- Freshly ground black pepper

In bowl of food processor or in a blender, combine the tofu, lemon juice, Dijon mustard, olive oil, nutritional yeast flakes, garlic, dill, salt, granulated onion, and turmeric. Blend well until the sauce is very smooth. There should be no lumps of tofu visible. Add additional salt (if necessary) and pepper to taste, blending again briefly.

Pour the sauce into a medium saucepan and place over medium-low heat. Whisk continuously, until the sauce is hot to the touch. Remove from heat and serve as needed.

If the sauce thickens too much after refrigeration, simply stir well and add a tablespoon of water or plain soymilk to thin as needed.

This sauce is fantastic over the Breakfast Benedicts Florentine, scrambled tofu, or even sliced ripe tomatoes.

Hollandaise Sauce
with Tarragon and White Wine

Growing up, Hollandaise sauce on Benedicts was
a favorite. After lots of experimenting, I came up with this delicious twist, making use of
silken tofu, fresh lemon juice, and tarragon. It makes one fantastic Benedict!

MAKES ABOUT 2 CUPS

- 1 (12-ounce) package silken tofu
- 3 tablespoons freshly squeezed lemon juice
- 3 tablespoons white wine
- 2 tablespoons plus 2 teaspoons nutritional yeast flakes
- 1 tablespoon fresh tarragon, chopped or 1 teaspoon dried
- 2 cloves garlic, pressed or minced
- 3 tablespoons non-hydrogenated vegan margarine, melted
- $^3/_4$ teaspoon fine sea salt, or to taste
- $^1/_8$ teaspoon ground turmeric
- Freshly ground black pepper

In the bowl of a food processor or in a blender, combine the tofu, lemon juice, white wine, nutritional yeast flakes, tarragon, and garlic. Blend for several minutes, until very smooth. There should be remaining lumps of tofu visible. Add the melted margarine, salt, and turmeric blending again until smooth. Add additional salt (if necessary) and pepper to taste, blending again briefly.

Pour the sauce into a medium saucepan and place over medium-low heat. Whisk the sauce continuously, until warmed through. Remove from heat and serve sauce over the prepared Breakfast Benedicts Florentine (page 48).

If the sauce thickens too much after refrigeration, simply stir well and add a tablespoon of water or plain soymilk to thin as needed.

Look for silken tofu in unrefrigerated aseptic boxes in supermarkets, health food stores, and Asian markets. I like using the Mori-Nu brand in this recipe, as it gives the sauce a truly silky texture.

Creamy Ranch Dressing

Ranch dressing is certainly the darling amongst
creamy salad dressings. I love the versatility of it; it goes on salads,
can be used as a dip, and is delicious on sandwiches.

MAKES ABOUT $^2/_3$ CUP

- 1/2 cup non-dairy sour cream
- 3 tablespoons unsweetened plain soymilk
- 1 tablespoon fresh lemon juice
- 1 teaspoon dried parsley or 1 tablespoon minced fresh parsley
- 1/2 teaspoon granulated garlic or garlic powder
- 1/2 teaspoon granulated onion or onion powder
- 1/2 teaspoon fine sea salt, or to taste
- 1/4 teaspoon freshly ground black pepper

In a medium bowl, whisk together the sour cream, soymilk, lemon juice, parsley, garlic, onion, salt, and pepper. Whisk until smooth and creamy.

Refrigerate the dressing for an hour, if possible, to let the flavors meld.

Variation: For a thicker ranch dip, omit the soymilk. For a Southwestern-style ranch, add a little bit of puréed canned chipotles in adobo sauce. Be careful because canned chipotles can be very hot. In place of the chipotles, add a few drops of hot sauce (such as Tapatío brand) to taste.

Creamy Tomato Dressing

Salads are one of the few ways that I can

easily get my son to eat his vegetables. Fortunately for me, he absolutely adores
the smoky flavors of this dressing on a spinach salad. This dressing can be made in
a flash, and is so much fresher-tasting than anything you can buy.

MAKES ABOUT 1 CUP

¹/₂ cup boiling water

¹/₄ cup lightly packed
sun-dried tomatoes (not
oil-packed)

6 tablespoons canola or
olive oil

1 tablespoon toasted
sesame oil

1 tablespoon balsamic
vinegar

3¹/₂ tablespoons nutritional
yeast flakes

2 large garlic cloves

¹/₂ teaspoon fine sea salt

In a small bowl, combine the boiling water and the sun-dried tomatoes, covering the dish with plastic wrap or foil. Let sit for 10 minutes, or until the tomatoes have softened.

In a blender jar, combine the sun-dried tomatoes and soaking liquid, canola oil, sesame oil, balsamic vinegar, nutritional yeast flakes, garlic, and salt. Blend mixture until ultra-smooth. Adjust seasonings to taste.

Use the dressing right away or transfer to a sealed container and store in the refrigerator.

Diner House Dressing

It's easy to forget how simple it is to make homemade dressings and keep them in your fridge, ready-to-go. This dressing is full of omega–3 fatty acids, and is a tasty way to eat your vegetables.

MAKES ABOUT ¹/₂ CUP

¹/₄ cup balsamic vinegar

2 tablespoons flax oil

2 tablespoons soy sauce

3 to 4 cloves garlic, pressed or finely minced

Kosher salt and freshly ground black pepper, to taste

In a bowl or glass jar, combine the balsamic vinegar, flax oil, soy sauce, garlic, and salt and pepper to taste. Whisk together until smooth.

Drizzle the dressing over salad greens or store in the refrigerator until ready to use.

Variation: Substitute hemp oil for the flax oil.

Flaxseed oil is considered one of the best plant-based sources of omega–3 fatty acids. Flax oil should never be heated, so it's a perfect oil to use in salad dressings and dips. Make sure to store your flax oil in the refrigerator, as it's very sensitive to light, heat, and oxygen.

Very Secret Sauce

Secret sauce is tangy and creamy, and creates
the magic on a great Reuben sandwich. This sauce will also work well on burgers or as a
French fry dipper. It will keep in your fridge for weeks, so feel free to double the recipe.

MAKES ABOUT 1¹/₄ CUPS

¹/₄ **cup ketchup**
¹/₂ **cup vegan mayo**
¹/₂ **tablespoon agave nectar**
Small pinch fine sea salt

In a bowl, whisk together the ketchup, mayo, and agave nectar until smooth and creamy. If needed, add a tiny pinch of salt.

Use the Secret Sauce right away, or transfer to a covered container and store in the refrigerator.

Tip: This recipe works really well with organic ketchup.

Variation: For a spicy kick, add a little cayenne or ground chipotle pepper.

I love making and creating sauces. They can add all sorts of new layers of flavors to sandwiches, burgers, and most everything else.

Cheezy Sauce

This sauce is a slight variation of the sauce
that I use for the Cheezy Mac. You'll love this sauce drizzled over French
fries, mashed potatoes, nachos, and just about everything.

MAKES ABOUT 2³/4 CUPS

2¹/₂ cups water

¹/₂ cup raw cashews

6 tablespoons nutritional
  yeast flakes

2 tablespoons cornstarch

2 tablespoons unbleached
  all-purpose flour

2 teaspoons granulated
  garlic or garlic powder

1¹/₂ teaspoons granulated
  onion or onion powder

1¹/₂ teaspoons smoked
  paprika

1¹/₄ teaspoons fine sea salt

1 teaspoon sweet or
  regular paprika

2 tablespoons non-
  hydrogenated vegan
  margarine, softened

In the jar of a blender, combine the water and cashews.
Blend mixture at high speed until completely smooth
and no bits of nuts remain. Add the nutritional yeast,
cornstarch, flour, garlic, onion, smoked paprika, salt,
and paprika, blending until very smooth.

Transfer the mixture to a large saucepan and place
over medium heat. Bring sauce to a simmer, whisking
continuously. Once mixture comes to a simmer, reduce
heat slightly and cook, whisking continuously until
thickened, about 3 to 5 minutes. Whisk in the margarine. If sauce is too thick, add a little additional water
to thin.

Use the sauce right away, or whisk it periodically until
it's cool. You want to keep a skin from forming on the
top of the sauce.

Variation: To make this a nacho cheezy sauce, increase
the granulated onion and smoked paprika to 2 teaspoons,
and add ¹/₄ teaspoon ground cumin. You can also stir in
chopped pickled jalapeños.

To give this sauce a touch of cheddary tang, stir in
2 teaspoons umeboshi vinegar into the cooked sauce.
Umboshi vinegar can be found in natural food stores and
Asian markets.

Great Smoky Mountain Cheeze

This is a creamy, spreadable cheese with a little bit of smokiness. It makes a fantastic grilled cheese sandwich! The cheese can be both sliced and spread, something that you can't say about dairy cheese!

MAKES 1 BLOCK

1/2 cup water, divided

2 teaspoons agar powder

1 (12.3 ounce) package silken firm or extra-firm tofu (preferably the Mori-Nu brand)

1/4 cup plus 2 tablespoons nutritional yeast flakes

3 tablespoons canola or other light flavorless oil

1 1/4 teaspoons fine sea salt

1 teaspoon smoked paprika

1/2 teaspoon granulated onion

1/2 teaspoon granulated garlic

1/2 teaspoon sweet or regular paprika

2 tablespoons plus 2 teaspoons cornstarch

Lightly grease a mini-loaf pan or glass or plastic rectangular or square container (see tip on next page). In a small bowl, mix together 1/4 cup water and the agar powder. Set aside for 5 minutes.

In bowl of food processor, combine the tofu, nutritional yeast flakes, oil, salt, smoked paprika, granulated onion, granulated garlic, and paprika. Blend for several minutes until very smooth, stopping to scrape down sides of the bowl as necessary.

In a small bowl, stir together the remaining 1/4 cup water with the cornstarch until smooth. Add the cornstarch mixture and the reserved agar mixture to the processor, and blend for 1 minute or until very smooth.

Transfer tofu mixture to a large saucepan. Quickly rinse out the food processor, as you'll need to blend the mixture again after cooking. Place saucepan over medium heat and cook, whisking continuously, until mixture starts to bubble. Reduce heat slightly if necessary. Continue cooking, whisking continuously, for another 2 to 3 minutes. This is necessary for the agar to melt completely. Reduce heat slightly if tofu mixture is starting to burn. Carefully transfer tofu mixture back to the food processor. Turn machine on and whiz until mixture is completely smooth, about 10 to 20 seconds.

Pour tofu mixture into prepared mold, smoothing top. Lightly tap mold on the countertop to settle the cheese, releasing any air bubbles. Place a piece of plastic wrap or waxed paper onto the top of the cheese mixture. This will prevent a skin from forming. Set aside

(continued on next page)

to cool down, about 20 minutes. Place the pan in the refrigerator and chill for several hours or overnight. Unmold cheese when ready to serve.

Tip: The size pan I use to mold the cheese is a $5^3/_4 \times 2^1/_2$-inch ceramic mini loaf pan (with a $2^1/_2$ cup capacity). You can also use a $1^1/_2$ cup plastic container which works well, too.

Agar powder is made from a seaweed and is used as a vegetarian gelatin. It's used extensively in Asia, especially in desserts. Look for agar powder in Asian markets and online. The powdered agar is much easier to use than the agar flakes, which is sometimes found in health food stores. The powder dissolves and cooks much quicker, and is also more potent, with a little going a long way. If you are only able to find the agar flakes, you can substitute 2 tablespoons flakes for the 2 teaspoons agar powder. Allow 7 to 8 minutes to cook instead of 2 to 3.

Garlic Dill Cheeze

It's so much fun to make your own vegan cheese at home.
This recipe is soft and spreadable: try it on crackers or a sandwich.

MAKES 1 BLOCK

2 teaspoons agar powder

1 (12.3 ounce) package silken firm tofu (preferably the Mori-Nu brand)

1/4 cup nutritional yeast flakes

3 tablespoons canola or other light flavorless oil

2 teaspoons granulated onion

2 teaspoons granulated garlic

1 1/4 teaspoons fine sea salt

2 tablespoons plus 2 teaspoons cornstarch

1 teaspoon dried dill weed

Lightly grease a mini-loaf pan or glass or plastic rectangular or square container (see tip on oppisite page). In a small bowl, mix together 1/4 cup water and the agar powder. Set aside for 5 minutes.

In bowl of food processor, combine the tofu, nutritional yeast flakes, oil, granulated onion, granulated garlic, and salt. Blend for several minutes until very smooth, stopping to scrape down sides of the bowl as necessary.

In a small bowl, stir together 1/4 cup water with the cornstarch until smooth. Add the cornstarch mixture and the reserved agar mixture to the processor, and blend for 1 minute or until very smooth. Add dried dill and pulse until well mixed.

Transfer tofu mixture to a large saucepan. Quickly rinse out the food processor, as you'll need to blend the mixture again after cooking. Place saucepan over medium heat and cook, whisking continuously, until mixture starts to bubble. Reduce heat slightly if necessary. Continue cooking, whisking continuously, for another 2 to 3 minutes. This is necessary for the agar to melt completely. Reduce heat slightly if tofu mixture is starting to burn. Carefully transfer tofu mixture back to the food processor. Turn machine on and whiz until mixture is completely smooth, about 10 to 20 seconds.

Pour tofu mixture into prepared mold, smoothing top. Lightly tap mold on the countertop to settle the cheese, releasing any air bubbles. Place a piece of plastic wrap onto the top of the cheese mixture. This will prevent a skin from forming. Set aside to cool down, about 20 minutes. Place the pan in the refrigerator and chill for several hours or overnight. Unmold cheese when ready to serve.

Homemade Garlic Mayo

This mayo is easy-peasy, thanks to the addition of
silken tofu. It's also heart-healthy, and is great in potato salads and on sandwiches.

MAKES ABOUT 2 CUPS

- 1 (12.3-ounce) package extra-firm silken tofu, preferably the Mori-Nu brand
- 3 tablespoons extra-virgin olive oil
- 3 tablespoons Dijon mustard
- 2 tablespoons freshly squeezed lemon juice
- 2 large cloves garlic
- $\frac{1}{2}$ teaspoon fine sea salt

In a food processor or blender, combine the tofu, olive oil, mustard, lemon juice, garlic, and salt. Purée tofu mixture until ultra smooth, stopping to scrape down the sides of the bowl or blender as necessary. Make sure that there aren't any little bits of unblended tofu.

Taste the mayonnaise, and adjust seasonings to taste. Transfer to a covered container and refrigerate for an hour, if possible, to let the flavors meld before using.

Tip: Don't use regular tofu for this recipe, as you won't get the lovely silky texture that you do from silken.

Variation: You can substitute whole grain mustard for the Dijon. You can also add another clove of garlic and a little freshly cracked pepper, for an extra zingy spread. For a lower fat mayo, reduce the olive oil to 2 tablespoons and use lite silken extra-firm tofu.

Mayo is one of those things that people can get very particular about. Some love it, same hate it, some like it slightly sweet, some tangy and some like it slathered on everything under the sun. I grew up in a family where the only mayo we ate was homemade with tons of fresh garlic. Of course the homemade stuff contained lots of egg yolks and cups of oil, while this version doesn't. Try it on sandwiches, as a dip for artichokes, or most anyplace that you would use store-bought mayo.

Mushroom–Pecan Sandwich Spread

This flavorful spread is wonderful on a sandwich,
especially with a good crusty bread. I like to think of this recipe as part diner,
part deli, or where the two worlds collide.

MAKES 2 CUPS

1 tablespoon extra-virgin
olive oil

1 large onion, diced

5 cups (12 ounces) sliced
cremini mushrooms,
rinsed and patted dry

1 teaspoon granulated sugar

1 cup raw pecans

2 tablespoons Marsala
or brandy

Fine sea salt and white
pepper, to taste

Sliced crusty bread,
for serving

Sliced sweet onions,
for serving

In a large skillet, heat the oil over medium-high heat. Add the onions and cook, stirring occasionally for 5 minutes. Add the mushrooms and cook for 10 to 15 minutes or until the liquid evaporates and the mushrooms and onions are soft and are lightly browning. Sprinkle the sugar over the mushroom mixture, and continue to cook until onions are caramelized, about another 3 to 5 minutes. Reduce heat as necessary so that the onions don't burn. Remove the skillet from the heat. Let the mixture cool for 5 minutes.

In bowl of food processor fitted with the metal blade, pulse the pecans until they are finely chopped. Add the mushroom mixture and the Marsala and blend until the mixture is smooth. Add salt and pepper to taste. Refrigerate mushroom mixture until ready to use.

To make sandwiches: Divide the Mushroom-Pecan Spread into fourths, and spread on 4 slices of good, crusty bread. Top with thinly sliced sweet onions and second slice of bread. You should have 4 sandwiches. For a sandwich variation, lightly toast the bread before assembling the sandwiches.

When I was young, I loved the flavors of caramelized onions in chopped liver, but wasn't too hot on the liver part. So when I became vegetarian, I started playing around with different versions of a mock spread, until I finally hit upon this one. One warning though: this stuff is utterly addictive.

Basil and Spinach Spread

Okay, this is really pesto, and it's probably

a bit out of place in a diner cookbook. But, truth be told, it works really well as a condiment to many of the recipes in this book, from grilled cheese and slider sandwiches to French fries and onion rings (as a dip, of course). So here you go.

MAKES 1 CUP

1 large handful fresh basil
leaves, about 2^1/$_8$ ounces,
washed and dried

1 large handful organic baby
spinach leaves, about 2
ounces, washed and dried

^{1}/$_3$ cup pine nuts or walnuts,
lightly toasted

3 to 4 large cloves garlic

^{1}/$_4$ teaspoon fine sea salt, or
to taste

^{1}/$_4$ cup extra-virgin olive oil

In the bowl of a food processor, combine the basil, spinach, pine nuts, garlic, and salt. Pulse to combine. Add the oil and process until smooth.

Fakin' Bakin' Bits

This recipe came from friend and cookbook author
Joni Marie Newman. Joni set out to find an alternative to the store–bought jars of fake
bacon bits, which are vegan but full of hydrogenated fats and dyes. This is a tasty
alternative and so easy to make, especially if you have liquid smoke on hand.

MAKES ABOUT 1 CUP

1/4 teaspoon fine sea salt

2 tablespoons liquid smoke

1 cup dried TVP or
   TSP granules

3 tablespoons canola or
   other vegetable oil

In a medium saucepan, add $7/8$ cup water plus the salt and bring to a boil over medium-high heat. Remove the saucepan from the heat.

Add liquid smoke to the hot water, mixing well. Add the granules to the hot water, stirring well. Cover the saucepan, and let stand for 10 minutes. Alternatively, in a microwave-safe dish, mix together the water, salt, liquid smoke, and TVP. Cover tightly with plastic wrap and microwave on high power for 5 to 6 minutes.

Set a frying pan over medium-high heat and add the oil. When the oil is hot, add the reconstituted granules to the pan and toss to make sure they all get coated with oil. Pan-fry until they are done to your liking, stirring them often, for about 10 minutes. You don't necessarily want to "brown" them, rather, dry them out. Allow to cool completely before transferring to an airtight container. Store in the refrigerator for a week or more.

Rich Brown Gravy

This fat-free and delicious brown gravy

will become a healthy staple. It's also wheat-free and nutritious. This recipe is
my variation of Bryanna Clark Grogan's Rich Brown Gravy recipe. Around my house,
this gravy is referred to as "crack gravy" because it's so addictive.

MAKES ABOUT 2¹/₂ CUPS

¹/₃ cup nutritional yeast
  flakes

2 tablespoons oat flour
  (grind-rolled or quick
  oats ground in a dry
  blender or spice mill)

4 tablespoons garbanzo
  bean flour

2¹/₂ cups water

2 tablespoons soy sauce

2 teaspoons granulated
  onion or onion powder

1 teaspoon granulated
  garlic or garlic powder

1 teaspoon dried parsley or
  1 tablespoon fresh minced
  parsley, optional

¹/₂ teaspoon dried rubbed
  sage

¹/₂ teaspoon salt, optional

Freshly ground black
  pepper, to taste

Ground white pepper,
  to taste

In a heavy saucepan over high heat, whisk together the
yeast, oat flour, and garbonzo flour, cooking until it
smells toasty. Remove the saucepan from the heat,
whisk in the water, soy sauce, onion, garlic, parsley,
sage, salt, and peppers, whisking until mixture is
smooth. Return saucepan to the heat, whisking con-
stantly over high heat until gravy thickens and comes
to a boil. Reduce the heat and simmer for about 5 minutes.

This gravy can be made ahead and reheated.

If you're looking for a gluten-free gravy, this is your
ticket. Just make sure to use wheat-free tamari and buy
certified gluten-free oat flour (or rolled oats and grind your
own flour in a blender or spice grinder).

Two-Pepper Golden Gravy

Sometimes there's nothing like a great gravy to liven up a dish, and this gravy is just the one to do it! Don't be surprised if you find yourself putting it on everything from toast to biscuits to seitan roasts.

MAKES ABOUT 1³/₄ CUPS

- ¹/₄ cup nutritional yeast flakes
- ¹/₄ cup unbleached all-purpose flour
- ¹/₄ cup chickpea flour
- 2 tablespoons soy sauce
- 1 cup plain unsweetened soymilk, plus more as needed
- ¹/₂ teaspoon fine sea salt, to taste
- ¹/₄ teaspoon white pepper, or to taste
- Freshly ground black pepper, to taste
- 1 tablespoon non-hydrogenated vegan margarine

In a medium saucepan, whisk together the nutritional yeast flakes, all-purpose flour, and chickpea flour. Add 2 cups water, whisking well until smooth. Whisk in the soy sauce, soymilk, salt, and peppers.

Bring mixture to a simmer over medium to medium-high heat, whisking continuously. Cook until gravy is thickened to desired consistency, whisking continuously, about 5 minutes. Add more soymilk as needed to thin.

Remove saucepan from heat and whisk in the margarine, adding additional salt and pepper to taste. Serve gravy right away while hot.

Tip: If you want to make this gravy gluten-free, one of my recipe testers discovered that it works really well to substitute ¹/₄ cup Bob's Red Mill All-Purpose Gluten-Free Flour for the ¹/₄ cup all-purpose flour called for in the recipe.

Rough Rider Barbecue Sauce

For years I found myself buying barbecue sauces,

not only because it's so easy to find at the store, but also because I just hadn't found a recipe I loved. Well, it all changed when I created this sweet and sticky barbecue sauce, and I can't imagine buying another one again. You'll be surprised at how easy this sauce is to make.

MAKES ABOUT 1 CUP

1 cup ketchup

$1/4$ cup agave nectar

$1/4$ cup light molasses

2 tablespoons cider vinegar

2 teaspoons soy sauce

2 teaspoons liquid smoke

$3/4$ teaspoon fresh ground black pepper

$1/2$ teaspoon granulated onion or onion powder

In a medium saucepan, whisk together all the ingredients plus $1/4$ cup water, whisking until smooth.

Over medium heat, bring mixture to a simmer. Reduce the heat to low and simmer, uncovered, stirring frequently for 30 minutes. For a really thick sauce, simmer an additional 15 minutes.

Let the sauce cool completely and refrigerate until ready to use.

Variation: For a spicier sauce, add about 1 teaspoon ground chipotle pepper to taste.

This recipe is even better when made with organic ketchup. Although any ketchup will work here, organic ketchup doesn't contain high-fructose corn syrup and tastes great.

Carolina-Style BBQ Sauce

There are so many different styles of BBQ sauce, and everyone has their own personal favorite. I really like adding a little drizzle of this very vinegary sauce along with lots of the Rough Rider Barbeque Sauce (see opposite page) on the Q sandwiches (page 96). It balances the sweetness of the Rough Rider Sauce, adding another dimension.

MAKES ABOUT 2 CUPS

1 cup cider vinegar

$1/4$ cup ketchup

$1/2$ cup water

2 tablespoons packed light brown sugar

$1 1/2$ teaspoons fine sea salt

$1/2$ teaspoon hot red pepper flakes

$1/2$ teaspoon freshly ground black pepper

In a medium container, whisk together the vinegar and ketchup until smooth.

In a small saucepan, heat the water, brown sugar, salt, red pepper flakes, and black pepper. Simmer just until sugar and salt are dissolved.

Remove from heat and add to the vinegar mixture, whisking until combined. Refrigerate until ready to use.

Tip: This sauce will keep refrigerated for weeks. I like to store it in a canning jar or an old salad dressing bottle.
I didn't grow up eating much ketchup, other than using it as a dip for fries or on a burger. But I've come to like it as an ingredient in BBQ sauce. So if you're leery of adding ketchup to your sauce, don't be. You can also reach for the organic versions, which are wonderful in the sauce recipes and can be found at most grocery and health food stores these days.

Cranberry Port Sauce

I love to serve cranberry sauce with seitan roast, mashed potatoes, and gravy, but it's also equally at home on top of a sliced seitan sandwich. Cranberries are also a great source of antioxidants. Although you may be tempted to cut down on the sugar in this recipe, it's a pretty tart sauce.

MAKES 2¼ CUPS

1 cup plus 2 tablespoons sugar, or a touch more to taste

1 cup port wine

1 (12-ounce) package fresh or frozen cranberries

Fresh grated zest and juice of 1 orange

Fresh grated zest and juice of 1 lemon

In a medium saucepan, combine the sugar, port wine, cranberries, orange zest and juice, and lemon zest and juice. Bring the mixture to a simmer over medium-high heat. Reduce heat slightly and simmer for 10 minutes or until thickened, stirring occasionally.

Remove the saucepan from heat and let the sauce cool. Serve or store in the refrigerator until ready to serve.

This sauce stores really well, so you can make it a couple of days before you want to serve it. This is especially helpful if you're cooking Thanksgiving dinner, and want to make some of the dishes ahead of time.

Resources

◆ ◆

Bob's Red Mill Natural Foods
www.bobsredmill.com
(800) 349-2173
A fantastic source for whole grain flours, grains, and beans.

Boyajian
www.boyajianinc.com
(800) 965-0665 or (781) 828-9966
They have a fabulous line of pure citrus oils, olive oils, and natural flavorings.

Cuisinart
www.cuisinart.com
Manufacturer of small kitchen appliances and cookware, including food processors, mixers, and ice cream makers.

Daiya
www.daiyafoods.com
They manufacture a line of vegan cheese, which tastes great and melts well.

Earth Balance
www.earthbalancenatural.com
A fantastic and flavorful line of non-hydrogenated vegan margarine.

Everyday Dish
www.everydaydish.tv
This website is home to our Everyday Dish Cooking Show and is a fun resource for vegan recipes.

Follow Your Heart
www.followyourheart.com
They make a great vegan mayonnaise, as well as vegan cheese, cream cheese, and sour cream.

Freddy Guy's Hazelnuts
www.freddyguys.com
(503) 606-0458
A hazelnut farm in Portland, Oregon. They have the freshest, most delicious hazelnuts I've ever tasted. They grow and roast their own hazelnuts.

Julie Hasson
www.juliehasson.com
This is my website and blog. You can also e-mail me your questions through the site.

KitchenAid
www.kitchenaid.com
Manufacturer of both small and large kitchen appliances, including food processors, mixers, and ranges.

Le Creuset
www.lecreuset.com

Manufacturer of excellent quality enameled cast-iron cookware, ceramic pie plates, mixing bowls, silicone spatulas, and much more.

Lodge
www.lodgemfg.com
(423) 837-7181
Manufacturer of excellent quality American-made cast-iron skillets and Dutch ovens.

Madhava
www.madhavahoney.com
(303) 823-5166
They have a great line of organic agave nectars.

Nielsen-Massey Vanillas
www.nielsenmassey.com
(847) 578-1550
Processor of high-quality pure vanilla extracts, beans, and powders, as well as a variety of other pure extracts.

Red Star
www.redstaryeast.com
A great website loaded with information about baking with yeast, the science of yeast, nutritional yeast, and more.

Soy Curls
www.butlerfoods.com
(503) 879-5005
Manufacturer of Soy Curls, a dry product made from the whole soybean.

The Soyfoods Council
www.thesoyfoodscouncil.com
The latest in soy research, plus recipes, tips, and more.

Tofutti
www.tofutti.com
A delicious brand of vegan cream cheese and sour cream.

Wholly Wholesome
www.whollywholesome.com
Manufacturer of excellent quality, organic, vegan frozen-pie shells and crumb crusts.

Index

Note: Page references in *italics* indicate photographs.